Artificial Intelligence for Social Good

Josh Cowls
Editor

Artificial Intelligence for Social Good

Previously published in *Philosophy & Technology* "Special Issue: Artificial Intelligence for Social Good" Volume 34, supplement issue 1, November 2021

Editor
Josh Cowls
Oxford Internet Institute
University of Oxford
Oxford, UK

Spinoff from journal: "Philosophy & Technology" Volume 34, supplement issue 1, November 2021

ISBN 978-3-031-18369-0

© The Editor(s) (if applicable) and The Author(s), under exclusive license to Springer Nature Switzerland AG 2022

Chapters "'AI for Social Good': Whose Good and Who's Good? Introduction to the Special Issue on Artificial Intelligence for Social Good", and "Testing the Black Box: Institutional Investors, Risk Disclosure, and Ethical AI" are licensed under the terms of the Creative Commons Attribution 4.0 International License (http://creativecommons.org/licenses/by/4.0/). For further details see license information in the chapters.

This work is subject to copyright. All rights are solely and exclusively licensed by the Publisher, whether the whole or part of the material is concerned, specifically the rights of translation, reprinting, reuse of illustrations, recitation, broadcasting, reproduction on microfilms or in any other physical way, and transmission or information storage and retrieval, electronic adaptation, computer software, or by similar or dissimilar methodology now known or hereafter developed.

The use of general descriptive names, registered names, trademarks, service marks, etc. in this publication does not imply, even in the absence of a specific statement, that such names are exempt from the relevant protective laws and regulations and therefore free for general use.

The publisher, the authors, and the editors are safe to assume that the advice and information in this book are believed to be true and accurate at the date of publication. Neither the publisher nor the authors or the editors give a warranty, expressed or implied, with respect to the material contained herein or for any errors or omissions that may have been made. The publisher remains neutral with regard to jurisdictional claims in published maps and institutional affiliations.

This Springer imprint is published by the registered company Springer Nature Switzerland AG
The registered company address is: Gewerbestrasse 11, 6330 Cham, Switzerland

Contents

'AI for Social Good': Whose Good and Who's Good? Introduction to the Special Issue on Artificial Intelligence for Social Good 1
J. Cowls: Philosophy & Technology 2021, 2021: 34 (Suppl 1):S1-S5 (13, August 2021) DOI: 10.1007/s13347-021-00466-3

Artificial Moral Agents Within an Ethos of AI4SG 7
B. A. Mabaso: Philosophy & Technology 2020, 2021: 34 (Suppl 1): S7-S21 (28, April 2020) DOI: 10.1007/s13347-020-00400-z

In the Frame: the Language of AI 23
H. Bones, S. Ford, R. Hendery, K. Richards, and T. Swist: Philosophy & Technology 2020, 2021: 34 (Suppl 1):S23-S44 (20, August 2020) DOI: 10.1007/s13347-020-00422-7

Artificial Interdisciplinarity: Artificial Intelligence for Research on Complex Societal Problems 45
S. D. Baum: Philosophy & Technology 2020, 2021: 34 (Suppl 1): S45-S63 (16, July 2020) DOI: 10.1007/s13347-020-00416-5

Engineering Equity: How AI Can Help Reduce the Harm of Implicit Bias 65
Y.-T. Lin, T.-W. Hung, and L. T. Huang: Philosophy & Technology 2020, 2021: 34 (Suppl 1):S65-S90 (3, July 2020) DOI: 10.1007/s13347-020-00406-7

Beyond a Human Rights-Based Approach to AI Governance: Promise, Pitfalls, Plea 91
N. A. Smuha: Philosophy & Technology 2020, 2021: 34 (Suppl 1): S91-S104 (24, May 2020) DOI: 10.1007/s13347-020-00403-w

Testing the Black Box: Institutional Investors, Risk Disclosure, and Ethical AI 105
T. Sanders: Philosophy & Technology 2020, 2021: 34 (Suppl 1): S105-S109 (24, July 2020) DOI: 10.1007/s13347-020-00409-4

How to Handle Armed Conflict Data in a Real-World Scenario? 111
A. Trivedi, K. Keator, M. Scholtens, B. Haigood, R. Dodhi, J. L. Ferres, R. Sankar, and A. Verma: Philosophy & Technology 2020, 2021: 34 (Suppl 1):S111-S123 (8, September 2020) DOI: 10.1007/s13347-020-00424-5

Philosophy & Technology (2021) 34 (Suppl 1):S1-S5
https://doi.org/10.1007/s13347-021-00466-3

RESEARCH ARTICLE

'AI for Social Good': Whose Good and Who's Good? Introduction to the Special Issue on Artificial Intelligence for Social Good

Josh Cowls[1,2]

Received: 14 July 2021 / Accepted: 31 July 2021 / Published online: 13 August 2021
© The Author(s) 2021

Abstract
This introduction sets out the aims and scope of the Special Issue and provides an overview of each of the research articles and commentaries that follow.

Keywords AI · Social good · AI for social good

Over the past decade, research into artificial intelligence (AI) has emerged from the shadow of a long winter of disregard into a balmy summer of hope and hype. Whilst scholars and advocates have studiously documented the risks and potential harms of deploying AI-based tools and techniques in an array of societal domains, the idea nonetheless persists that the promised power of AI functionally could and ethically should be harnessed for, or at least (re-)oriented towards, 'socially good' purposes.

The twin aims of this Special Issue, simply stated, are to interrogate the plausibility of this notion and to consider its implications. The case that AI may — if developed carefully and deployed sensitively (Floridi et al., 2020) — contribute to net-positive outcomes in (some) socially relevant spheres is not without foundation. An array of efforts and initiatives are already underway, for example, to develop AI-based responses to help meet the UN's Sustainable Development Goals (SDGs) by 2030 (Cowls et al., 2021; Vinuesa et al., 2020). And as the suddenness of the Covid pandemic and the rapidity of global climate change both serve to remind us, global society faces challenges so stark and all-encompassing that an 'all-of-the-above' attitude towards potential solutions — especially those with a silicon sheen — may prove irresistible. Yet the susceptibility to the allure of technological solutions that increasing societal vulnerability engenders ought to give all of us pause, for reasons of both practice and of principle.

Chapter 1 was originally published as Cowls, J. Philosophy & Technology 2021) 34 (Suppl 1):S1-S5. https://doi.org/10.1007/s13347-021-00466-3.

✉ Josh Cowls
josh.cowls@oii.ox.ac.uk

[1] Oxford Internet Institute, University of Oxford, Oxford, UK

[2] Alan Turing Institute, London, UK

Reprinted from the journal   1   ◯ Springer

In practical terms, it is only when the haze of hype that surrounds AI is cut through that we can begin to consider the actual benefits and costs of specific AI-based tools, deployed in specific domains, developed for specific purposes. AI as a term operates as useful rhetorical flypaper for politicians looking to establish their twenty-first century policymaking credentials, as much as for start-ups on the search for seed-funding — and overstating the potential of AI serves the interests of both constituencies, and many others, well. It therefore seems prudent to adopt a cautious, evidence-based attitude towards claims made about the potential positive impact of AI, whether in the private, public, or non-profit spheres.

The prospect of AI for social good also invites more principled questions. The recent wave of AI hype has coincided not only with historically stark social challenges, but also at a time in which a small handful of private technology companies occupy a dominant position in many walks of life. Many of these companies have developed AI for use, first and foremost, in the day-to-day operation of their products and services, from predicting consumer preferences and recommending videos to driving autonomous vehicles and detecting atrial fibrillation. Several of them have also created units explicitly dedicated to using AI for socially good purposes. The active involvement of these for-profit companies in avowedly 'good' initiatives, as well as, for example, the embrace of similar efforts by governments both democratic and autocratic, points to the broader questions of whose 'good' is being served by projects branded as AI for social good, and who may be called 'good' as a result of such efforts.

Such questions are not novel. Moore (2019), for example, has explored the meaning and implications of 'AI for social good' and argues instead for 'AI for not bad', citing the vagueness and critical inadequacy of the term, bringing to mind Taylor's (2016) question regarding whose good is meant to be served by the use of big data as a 'public good'. But addressing these questions more fully — about whose good is served by, and who ought to be thought of as good as a result of, AI for social good — benefits from the series of empirically and ethically grounded contributions that are assembled in this Special Issue.

In 'Artificial Moral Agents Within in Ethos of AI4SG', Bongani Andy Mabaso asks which ethical framework artificial agents should be obliged to follow. Mabaso makes the case for exemplarism, a theory based on virtue ethics, as just such a framework, identifying several key features of exemplarism that 'fit the ethos of AI4SG'. These include exemplarism's conceptual grounding within existing exemplars of moral goodness, and the framework's responsiveness to societal expectations. Mabaso provides an example of an artificial agent deployed in an educational context, notes ongoing challenges to the teaching and learning of moral behaviour from exemplars and concludes by arguing that an exemplarist-based artificial agent may already be technologically possible if developed for carefully selected social contexts where relevant data is available.

The article 'In the Frame: the Language of AI', by Bones and co-authors, focuses attention on the discourses and practices associated with AI4SG. They employ a feminist epistemology to engage critically with the language most frequently used to characterise AI. Through a hybrid of historical, textual and corpus linguistic approaches, they show how the affordances and constraints of several key terms adjacent to AI, like 'data', 'memory' and 'intelligence', help to shape non-expert understanding of what AI is and what it could be. Reframing AI for social good, they argue, is therefore in part a matter of making more careful, sensitive choices with respect to the language used to convey AI's potential and limitations, eschewing euphemism, hype and dogma. True AI4SG rests, therefore, on the facilitation of more inclusive and representative conversations which draw on an improved vocabulary and a more informed sense of what direction the deployment of AI could and should take.

In 'Artificial Interdisciplinarity: Artificial Intelligence for Research on Complex Societal Problems', Seth D. Baum explores a potential intersection between AI, interdisciplinary research and complex social problems. As Baum notes, much present AI work is oriented towards goals of expanding AI's technological capacity and increasing the profits of technology companies, whilst interdisciplinary research is far from a panacea for solving social challenges and can sometimes be outright harmful to societal interests. Whilst, as Baum acknowledges, there are already several ways in which AI systems facilitate interdisciplinary research, such as search engines and recommendation systems, there are several more tasks they could be designed to do, especially in the medium term, in support of interdisciplinary research. Yet Baum also anticipates the difficulties and risks that may arise from such a programme of development, some of which emerge from the risks of AI more generally, and others which arise as result of the high societal stakes of interdisciplinary research in areas such as global climate change and nuclear power.

In their research article 'Engineering Equity: How AI Can Help Reduce the Harm of Implicit Bias', Ying-Tung Lin, Tzu-Wei Hung and Linus Ta-Lun Huang explore AI in the context of implicit bias. Whilst acknowledging existing evidence suggesting that AI can perpetuate bias, the authors provide a framework within which to consider the use of AI to actively reduce the harms of implicit bias. Using recruitment processes as a case study, they highlight several areas in which using AI could potentially be of benefit, both with respect to the different information that AI provides to human users, and regarding the interventions that AI systems can be designed to make to reduce harms. Whilst the interventions proposed here apply primarily at the level of individual cognitive biases, the authors argue that they could form part of a package of responses that — along with structural changes — can serve the common interest of reducing the harms of implicit bias.

The Issue concludes with a series of commentaries considering other elements of AI in the context of social good. In 'Beyond a Human Rights-Based Approach to AI Governance: Promise, Pitfalls, Plea', Nathalie A. Smuha considers the ethical and political implications of taking a human rights-based approach to a governance framework for good AI. Writing against the backdrop of the European Commission's High-Level Expert Group and its charge to develop guidelines and recommendations for EU policymaking, Smuha discusses the search for a moral compass to guide the future directions of AI governance. Though acknowledging that human rights are neither flawless nor free of contestation, Smuha nonetheless advocates, persuasively, for the adoption of a human rights framework as the compass to steer AI governance in societally 'good' directions.

Meanwhile, Trooper Sanders' commentary, 'Testing the Black Box: Institutional Investors, Risk Disclosure, and Ethical AI', considers the role of institutional investors in advancing the development of responsible AI. Sanders notes that pushing for greater transparency in how AI is designed and deployed on the part of investors can involve both emboldening regulators and assessing the ethical fitness of companies in their portfolio. Drawing on lessons from the environmental, social and governance investing movement, Sanders outlines several ways in which 'institutional investors could give the ethical AI field some essential oomph'. Sanders thus identifies a potentially impactful front in the push to ensure that AI benefits society.

Finally, in their commentary, 'How to Handle Armed Conflict Data in a Real-World Scenario?', Trivedi and co-authors assess the utility of deep natural language processing to transform data from armed conflicts for the benefit of conflict resolution practitioners. Introducing a model initially trained on conflict data from Syria, the authors report a high degree of accuracy in the automated classifications of specific events that occurred between 2018 and 2019. Noting that there is no 'one-size-fits-all' model for classification tasks of this sort, given the complexity and context-specificity of armed conflict, the authors argue that sensitively constructed models like the one they introduce could give conflict resolution practitioners more time to conduct other essential analyses and collect more data.

Taken together, the research articles and commentaries that constitute this Special Issue provide an array of distinct perspectives that address both the plausibility and implications of AI4SG in particular settings and contexts. The contributions make clear that neither 'AI' nor 'social good' should be thought of as uncontested or incontestable terms, and we should remain wary of the twin dangers of unjustified hype and unseen harm arising from the continued growth of interest in, and application of, AI. Yet at what is a time of great vulnerability for a great many, undoubtedly there remain numerous domains in which sensitively designed systems utilising some form of artificial intelligence may help meet the pressing needs of societies and communities of practice around the world.

Open Access This article is licensed under a Creative Commons Attribution 4.0 International License, which permits use, sharing, adaptation, distribution and reproduction in any medium or format, as long as you give appropriate credit to the original author(s) and the source, provide a link to the Creative Commons licence, and indicate if changes were made. The images or other third party material in this article are included in the article's Creative Commons licence, unless indicated otherwise in a credit line to the material. If material is not included in the article's Creative Commons licence and your intended use is not permitted by statutory regulation or exceeds the permitted use, you will need to obtain permission directly from the copyright holder. To view a copy of this licence, visit http://creativecommons.org/licenses/by/4.0/.

References

Cowls, J., Tsamados, A., Taddeo, M., & Floridi, L. (2021). A definition, benchmark and database of AI for social good initiatives. *Nature Machine Intelligence, 3*(2), 111–115. https://doi.org/10.1038/s42256-021-00296-0

Floridi, L., Cowls, J., King, T. C., & Taddeo, M. (2020). How to design AI for social good: Seven essential factors. *Science Engineering and Ethics*. https://doi.org/10.1007/s11948-020-00213-5

Moore, Jared. (2019). AI for not bad. *Front Big Data, 2*, 32. https://doi.org/10.3389/fdata.2019.00032

Taylor, L. (2016). The ethics of big data as a public good: Which public? Whose good? *Philosophical Transactions of the Royal Society a: Mathematical, Physical and Engineering Sciences, 374*(2083), 20160126. https://doi.org/10.1098/rsta.2016.0126

Vinuesa, R., Azizpour, H., Leite, I., Balaam, M., Dignum, V., Domisch, S., Felländer, A., Langhans, S. D., Tegmark, M., & Nerini, F. F. (2020). The role of artificial intelligence in achieving the sustainable development goals. *Nature Communications, 11*(1), 1–10. https://doi.org/10.1038/s41467-019-14108-y

Publisher's Note Springer Nature remains neutral with regard to jurisdictional claims in published maps and institutional affiliations.

Philosophy & Technology (2021) 34 (Suppl 1):S7-S21
https://doi.org/10.1007/s13347-020-00400-z

RESEARCH ARTICLE

Artificial Moral Agents Within an Ethos of AI4SG

Bongani Andy Mabaso[1]

Received: 30 September 2019 / Accepted: 30 March 2020 / Published online: 28 April 2020
© Springer Nature B.V. 2020

Abstract
As artificial intelligence (AI) continues to proliferate into every area of modern life, there is no doubt that society has to think deeply about the potential impact, whether negative or positive, that it will have. Whilst scholars recognise that AI can usher in a new era of personal, social and economic prosperity, they also warn of the potential for it to be misused towards the detriment of society. Deliberate strategies are therefore required to ensure that AI can be safely integrated into society in a manner that would maximise the good for as many people as possible, whilst minimising the bad. One of the most urgent societal expectations of artificial agents is the need for them to behave in a manner that is morally relevant, i.e. to become artificial moral agents (AMAs). In this article, I will argue that exemplarism, an ethical theory based on virtue ethics, can be employed in the building of computationally rational AMAs with weak machine ethics. I further argue that three features of exemplarism, namely grounding in moral exemplars, meeting community expectations and practical simplicity, are crucial to its uniqueness and suitability for application in building AMAs that fit the ethos of AI4SG.

Keywords Exemplarism · AI4SG · Machine ethics · Artificial moral agency

1 Introduction

As artificial intelligence (AI) continues to proliferate into every area of modern life, there is no doubt that society has to think deeply about the potential impact, whether negative or positive, that it will have. Whilst scholars recognise that AI can usher in a new era of personal, social and economic prosperity (Aghion et al. 2017), they also warn of the potential for it to be misused towards the detriment of society (Alzahrani 2016). Deliberate strategies are therefore required to ensure that AI can be safely

---

Chapter 2 was originally published as Mabaso, B. A. Philosophy & Technology (2021) 34 (Suppl 1):S7-S21.
https://doi.org/10.1007/s13347-020-00400-z.

✉ Bongani Andy Mabaso
   bamabaso@gmail.com

[1] University of Pretoria, Pretoria, South Africa

introduced and integrated into society in a manner that would maximise the good for as many people as possible, whilst minimising the bad.

Scholars, organisations and policymakers have begun gravitating towards using the acronym AI4SG, which stands for "AI for social good", to capture the ethos of all those that are involved at various levels in ensuring that AI can be used in a manner that would promote human flourishing. Cowls and Floridi (2018) capture the opportunities in AI4SG well by pointing out that it can lead to human self-actualisation, increased agency, better social capabilities and greater societal cohesion. They also warn, however, that misuse or overuse of AI could also lead to the detrimental effects of loss of human control and agency, devalued human skills and an eroded potential for human determination. It is in the best interest of society to mitigate these risks.

For this article, I will focus on the risks of loss of human control and agency. I want to relate these risks to the familiar challenge in machine ethics of "developing computer systems and robots capable of making moral decisions" (Allen and Wallach 2011). Many philosophers and ethicists have raised concerns about how increasingly autonomous artificial agents will treat human beings, and whether this treatment will be ethical (Moor 2006; Dameski 2018; Allen and Wallach 2011; Anderson and Anderson 2007). If these artificial agents are deployed into society without the necessary measures to deal with morally charged situations, the risks of loss of human control and agency may often materialise.

There is a strong philosophical foundation to suggest that the artificial moral agent (AMA) project is at least theoretically achievable (Abney 2012; Scheutz and Malle 2017; Floridi and Sanders 2004; Sullins 2006; Moor 2006; Johnson 2006). There are also many projects that have demonstrated some practical viability of building AMAs, such as the works of Cloos (2005), Wallach et al. (2010), Anderson and Anderson (2011), Pontier and Hoorn (2012), and Howard and Muntean (2016). A core idea that often goes unexpressed, but is foundational in many of these works, is that computational rationality (Simon 1955; Horvitz 1987; Gershman et al. 2015) can entail artificial moral agency.

Computational rationality alone, however, is not sufficient to build AMAs. We still need to choose or design an ethical framework that the AMA ought to follow. So which one should the AMA follow? It is vital to address this question because as members of society, we want to ensure that artificial agents will behave in a manner that is consistent with our communal expectations of moral behaviour. The ethos of AI4SG needs to be applicable, maybe even more so, when it comes to how increasingly autonomous artificial agents will treat us (Moor 2006).

In this article, I want to show how exemplarism, an ethical theory based on virtue ethics, can be employed in the building of computationally rational AMAs with weak machine ethics. I further argue that three features of exemplarism, namely *grounding in moral exemplars*, *meeting community expectations* and *practical simplicity*, are crucial to its uniqueness and suitability for application in building AMAs that fit the ethos of AI4SG. Furthermore, I will also paint a detailed scenario that will seek to demonstrate how exemplarism might practically work in an AMA.

2 Artificial Moral Agency

Depending on how the concept of moral agency is framed, we may end up with a concept that either includes or excludes artificial agents in the moral universe. A helpful way that I have found to frame the concept is by looking at moral agents through three lenses. These lenses are *biological moral agency* (Torrance 2008; Churchland 2014; Liao 2010; Rottschaefer 2000); *conscious moral agency* (Parthemore and Whitby 2013; 2014; Himma 2008); and *artificial moral agency* (Abney 2012; Scheutz and Malle 2017; Floridi and Sanders 2004; Sullins 2006; Moor 2006; Johnson 2006).

Biological moral agency is an argument that agents need to be necessarily biological to qualify as moral agents. It further argues that all the capacities and requirements for moral agency (consciousness, emotions, free will, etc.) are fundamentally derived from the agent's biological nature (Torrance 2008). If we view moral agency through this lens, then computationally based artificial agents would not qualify as moral agents.

Conscious moral agency is an argument that agents need to be conscious to qualify as moral agents. All the capacities and requirements for moral agency are derived from the agent's consciousness. Note that conscious moral agents need not necessarily be biological! (Parthemore and Whitby 2013, 2014). If we view moral agency through this lens, then most (if not all) artificial agents would not qualify as moral agents.

Artificial moral agency is an argument that agents can be built to either simulate the required epistemic capacities for moral agency or mimic moral behaviours such that the agent qualifies as an artificial moral agent. This view includes artificial agents in the moral universe, and it is the default lens to apply when thinking about building AMAs.

Artificial moral agency can be further looked at from two lenses. Firstly, a lens that suggests most, if not all, of the full range of moral decisions can be computed by some near or future term artificial agent (Abney 2012; Sullins 2006; Allen and Wallach 2011). Secondly, a lens that suggests only certain kinds of moral decisions can be made using computational approaches to AI, and that the full range of moral decisions will require super-rational capacities (Scheutz and Malle 2017; Johnson 2006). I call the former lens *strong machine ethics*, and the latter *weak machine ethics*.

I adopt a weak machine ethics lens in this article because I believe it aligns more closely with what is possible in the current state of the art of AI. Furthermore, I believe it helps us avoid the trap of focusing too much on building AMAs that rival human moral competence at the expense of building them to respond to the current ethical challenges of making "increasingly autonomous robots safer and more respecting of moral values, given present or near-future technology" (Allen and Wallach 2011).

Another benefit of choosing a weak machine ethics lens is its compatibility with computational rationality. Computational rationality is about finding ways of making rational decisions in computerised systems despite the apparent algorithmic, computational and informational limitations (Simon 1955; Horvitz 1987; Gershman et al. 2015). In other words, it is about making rational decisions within the current state of the art of computing—something that fits the framing of weak machine ethics well.

3 Machine Ethics Frameworks

Before I discuss exemplarism in detail, I want to briefly mention the three main ethical theories[1] that philosophers and designers have considered for use in the AMA project (Gips 1995). This brief discussion is essential for two reasons. Firstly, an understanding of the theories will help designers of AMAs in making the right choices when it comes to constructing a machine ethics framework for their project(s). Secondly, it will bring context to the discussion on exemplarism, especially since it is a derivative of virtue ethics, which is one of the three ethical theories.

Consequentialist approaches to machine ethics have to do with linking the morality of an action to its outcome (Dignum 2017; Scheutz and Malle 2017; Gips 1995; Kuipers 2016). The outcomes are viewed from a perspective of consequences, with those that maximise good or happiness being more ethical than those that do not. As Scheutz and Malle (2017) note, consequentialist approaches are perhaps closest to the general computational mechanisms that already exist in fields such as robotics, AI and control systems. This is because many of these mechanisms are based on utility theories which tend to favour actions or activities that maximise (or minimise) certain pre-selected variables. Utilitarianism, perhaps the most well-known form of consequentialism, works on a similar principle to maximise the overall utility (happiness or good) of everyone involved.

Deontological approaches to machine ethics have to do with designing AMAs that can do what is right (Dignum 2017; Scheutz and Malle 2017; Gips 1995; Kuipers 2016). What is right can be the performance of a duty for the AMA itself, society or even the environment. In the general sense, it can be about knowing and performing specific universal rules (such as Kant's categorical imperative). In a more defined context, it can be about performing specifically assigned duties that are accepted as objective or established norms. In contrast to consequentialist approaches, deontological approaches to machine ethics are not primarily concerned with outcomes of the actions. Instead, they are concerned with the "rightness", and inversely the "wrongness", of the AMA actions.

Classical Aristotelian virtue ethics has to do with living a life based on virtues (compassion, generosity, honesty, etc.), which leads to the attainment of "happiness", or "eudaimonia".[2] It focuses on life-long character development of virtues and minimising vices in one's life. A person is considered ethical if they are able to act in a

---

[1] The three main ethical theories in normative ethics are consequentialism, deontology and virtue ethics.
[2] Often translated from Greek to English as "happiness", "flourishing", "well-being" or even the "good life".

manner that is consistent with how a virtuous person would have acted in a given scenario. Just being virtuous, however, is not necessarily enough to live the "good life", a person also has to have moral or practical wisdom, phronesis, to attain eudaimonia (Miller 1984; Annas 2011). Practical wisdom is the ability to know when, and how much, one should act based on which virtues, because blind virtue can also lead to a fault!

A virtue approach to machine ethics is therefore not primarily about what actions are right, or which lead to the greatest amount of good. It is instead about striving to become a certain kind of artificial agent. It emphasises the artificial agent's "life-long" approach to character building and a constant striving to becoming virtuous (Abney 2012).

4 Exemplarism in AMAs

Exemplarist virtue ethics, or simply exemplarism, is a moral theory that was proposed and developed by Linda Zagzebski (2010). In contrast to classical virtue ethics, exemplarism is not conceptually grounded in virtues or achieving eudaimonia. Instead, it is grounded in the *exemplars of moral goodness* (Zagzebski 2010). Exemplarism often gets classified under agent-based virtue ethics, another derivative of classical virtue ethics (Slote 1995; Hursthouse and Pettigrove 2018); however, I will discuss exemplarism independently of agent-based virtue ethics in this article.

Zagzebski defines the exemplars of moral goodness as morally admirable agents whose example is worth following. All other moral concepts are then grounded on the exemplars of moral goodness. For example, an agent would desire to be virtuous because an exemplar of moral goodness is virtuous. Since exemplarism is about following the example of morally admirable agents in society, exemplarist agents, therefore, need to be good at identifying them, something that Zagzebski (2010) states can be achieved through empirical observation.

It is important to state here that my application of exemplarism does not forego the need for practical wisdom in the making of moral decisions—it is still based on classical Aristotelian virtue ethics. However, where Aristotelian virtue ethics is conceptually grounded in the virtues of a good life, exemplarism is practically grounded in exemplars of moral goodness.

In other words, my application of Linda Zagzebski's theory is not merely about building AMAs that blindly follow examples of morally worthy agents in society. Instead, it is about learning how these morally worthy individuals make moral decisions, whilst still retaining the critical capacity for making independent moral decisions—something that is a definite requirement for artificial moral agency (Floridi and Sanders 2004). In the end, the AMA would still need to choose computationally rational moral decisions.[3]

---

[3]From a design perspective, this would mean using a learning-based approach to form an internal representation of moral values and a completely different decision-making procedure to make moral decisions. This is similar in approach to how Howard and Muntean (2016) designed their AMA, although they have slightly different reasons for using this technique.

I am now going to discuss three key features of exemplarism that make it uniquely suited to building AMAs that fit the ethos of AI4SG. The first feature has to do with the conceptual grounding of exemplarism. The second feature has to do with meeting community expectations. The third and last feature has to do with its practicality. I will discuss each of these features next.

Conceptual Grounding of Exemplarism Classical virtue ethics is conceptually grounded in virtues. For a human being, this kind of conceptual grounding is not generally problematic, but for an AMA conceptualised with weak machine ethics, it can be a big problem. How does one go about computationally modelling virtues? If we take a virtue such as courage, what would that look like in an AMA? What about all the other virtues such as temperance, honesty and compassion? Clearly, there are computational limitations to building the understanding of highly abstract concepts into AMAs.

Exemplarism, on the other hand, is not grounded in abstract concepts, but in the exemplars of moral goodness. The implication of this is quite straightforward—the AMA only has to follow the examples of morally upright agents to learn an implicit representation of society's moral values. The difference between this and the other forms of virtue ethics is subtle, but it is there. From a purely computational perspective, the problem of learning from example is more readily solvable than programming the understanding of abstract concepts into the AMA.

Note that I am not saying this is trivial—it is still difficult and it has its challenges! However, if empirical observation is how one identifies and learns from moral exemplars (Zagzebski 2010), then this strongly suggests that an AMA can also identify and learn from moral exemplars. Once the AMA has learned an implicit internal representation of moral values, it can then proceed to apply it (through its computational rationality) to make decisions in morally charged situations.

Exemplarism Can Meet Community Expectations Moral introspection is a strength, rather than a weakness, of virtue ethics approaches. However, it can be a weakness if the AMA is so wholly disconnected from (societal) reality in its moral decision making. It seems to me that to be a good exemplarist moral agent, one needs a kind of "golden mean"[4] between internal introspection about moral decisions and an external grasp of how the most admirable moral exemplars in society behave. This golden mean, I suggest, ensures that the exemplarist AMA is both responsive to societal moral values whilst remaining autonomous in its final decision making (Floridi and Sanders 2004).

In exemplarism, virtue does not have to be learned and understood directly—it is indirectly learned through the admiration and following of moral exemplars in society. I argue that this is more desirable for a weak machine ethics AMA because it is achievable, and the outcomes are aligned to community expectations. In the end, exemplarism seems not only to bypass the problem of directly modelling highly

---

[4] Aristotle believed that a person needs a balance between the vices of deficiency and excess to be virtuous. This balance can be thought of as a conceptual mid-point between two opposite vices—a "golden mean".

abstract concepts like virtues, but it also meets community expectations by following those same agents that society would hold up high as moral examples. This is why I say that it lies at the golden mean of virtue ethics approaches.

I am aware of a criticism that states that AMAs cannot achieve community expectations of moral behaviour by learning an aggregated view of societal moral value because one does not exist (Baum 2017). Interestingly, Zagzebski (2010) formulates her theory in a way that shows that she is aware of this broad criticism that can be laid against it due to its apparent divorce of a descriptive understanding of virtues in moral choice.

Zagzebski (2010) argues using the theory of direct reference to say that people have always been able to refer to terms such as gold or water before they knew how gold or water was composed atomically. Similarly, she argues that it is possible to fix a reference for moral values without necessarily having a descriptive understanding of them. By implication, people can identify good or bad moral exemplars without necessarily being able to define the virtues or vices that make them good or bad.

If we apply Zagzebski's thinking to AMAs, then they too can learn an approximation of an aggregated view of societal moral value by direct reference, especially when learning from many exemplars. AMAs can determine that an individual is likely a good or bad exemplar, and this information can be aggregated across the entire population of exemplars.

While I cannot exhaustively discuss the concept of value alignment in AMAs here, I point the reader to the works of Vamplew et al. (2018) and Prasad (2018), who have dealt with the topic more comprehensively. I also refer the reader to the next section, where I seek to practically demonstrate how exemplarist AMAs might learn from exemplars to meet community expectations of moral behaviour in a specific scenario.

Exemplarism Can Be Practical From a machine ethics point of view, exemplarism is a pragmatic approach to building AMAs because the goal is at least conceptually and practically clear—teach AMAs to learn from moral exemplars and to improve themselves over time. If we assume, as Zagzebski (2010) does, that moral values can be learned through empirical observation, then this would imply that many current techniques in AI could be applied to at least partially implement the AMA. I am aware that collecting data through observation is tricky, but at least we are dealing with a problem that is understood and for which some attempts at solving have been made (Duan et al. 2017; Howard and Muntean 2016). I argue that this conceptual simplicity likely makes the task of actually programming exemplarism into an AMA feasible, as I will demonstrate in the next section.

The three features of exemplarism that I have just discussed, namely *grounding in moral exemplars*, *meeting community expectations* and *practical simplicity*, are what makes it stand out as a choice of ethical theory to support the building of AMAs that meet the ethos of AI4SG. Note, I make this conclusion in the context of building exemplarist AMAs that are conceptualised to have weak machine ethics—different conclusions would likely be reached if the underlying assumptions are changed.

5 How It Can Work: Exemplarism in Action

My main aim in the previous section was to introduce exemplarism and position it as a viable alternative ethical theory to support the AMA project. I do, however, admit that such an introduction will be inherently insufficient, especially in such a short article. That is why the purpose of this section is to give a scenario that would demonstrate how it might work in practice. The hope is that this will further clarify key concepts in my application of exemplarism, and generally make it more practical for the reader.

Since I am dealing with weak machine ethics (see Section 2), it makes sense to constrain my scenario to a specific context where I can explore how exemplarism in AMAs might work in practice. This is similar to how the field of applied ethics attempts to study and apply ethics in specific contexts such as business, environmental, medical, educational and wartime ethics. At a minimum, the scenario would need to demonstrate how the AMA might identify moral exemplars, learn moral behaviour and make moral decisions.

Imagine a near-future classroom that is taught by a robotic teacher (call it Robo-teacher). Robo-teacher is responsible for teaching mathematics to 20 students from diverse cultures and socio-economic backgrounds. One student in particular (call them Nancy) is quite disruptive in class and has historically caused Robo-teacher to spend an inordinate amount of time focusing on her, at the expense of the other learners. Robo-teacher reported the issue to the headmaster, who immediately sought the help of its manufacturer and tasked them with equipping Robo-teacher with the ability to handle ethical situations in the classroom.[5]

The manufacturer decides to use exemplarism as the ethical theory of choice and builds it into the ethical routine of Robo-teacher. For Robo-teacher to handle the situation with Nancy appropriately when next it happens, it needs to do three things. Firstly, it needs to identify morally praiseworthy teachers in the school, district or even nationally. Secondly, it needs to learn how these same teachers handle classroom ethics, and in particular similar situations in their contexts. Lastly, it needs to use the knowledge to decide on an appropriate action to perform.

There are multiple ways in which Robo-teacher could identify moral exemplars (e.g. physically observing many teachers whilst they teach, searching the internet for exemplar teacher cases and stories, simply being told). For this scenario, I will assume that the manufacturer has kept a database of teachers (good or bad) for use in training their robot teachers and that this database remains available to Robo-teacher even after it is deployed to a school. Additionally, this database contains a numeric indicator of how effective the teacher has been at dealing with morally charged situations in the classroom, perhaps using a combination of teacher, learner and parental feedback.

Zagzebski states that people "identify admirable persons by the emotion of admiration, and that emotion is itself subject to education through the example of the

---

[5]This scenario is mostly based on a collection of case studies on classroom ethics by Levinson and Fay (2016). I have merely replaced the human teacher with Robo-teacher in the scenario, and used different names for the student(s).

emotional reactions of other persons" (Zagzebski 2010, p. 52). Robo-teacher does not have the "emotion of admiration", but it can search the database and look for examples of teachers that have had relative success based on the numeric indicator mentioned above. It could also use other indicators, like the number of learners in a class, the area in which the teacher was based, the grade of the class and even specific cases to help it to hone in on the right exemplars to learn from.

The next task is for Robo-teacher to learn a system of moral values from the identified exemplar teachers. The good thing about picking specific contexts (in this case, a classroom) is that it makes the task of knowledge engineering far easier, and possible (Russell and Norvig 2009).[6] On top of the database of exemplars discussed above, the classroom context also makes it possible to place various sensors in the room to pick up sound, determine who is seated or talking, etc. The classroom sessions can also be video recorded so that a rich dataset of exemplar teachers conducting lessons and interacting with learners is available. This sensor and video data could be used to enhance the repository of information available further and to teach robot teachers about classroom ethics.

For this scenario, I am proposing that Robo-teacher uses a bottom-up approach to learn a system of moral values that would be appropriate for classroom ethics. This means that Robo-teacher would use the various types of data available to learn, through an appropriately designed machine learning approach, from numerous and diverse exemplar teachers conducting classroom sessions.

This will allow it to form a general representation of ethical behaviour that is appropriate for a teacher in a classroom setting. Learning from many exemplars ensures that Robo-teacher does not merely parrot learn from one or a few examples, but that it bases its moral knowledge on a wide variety of scenarios and exemplar teachers. Furthermore, it is important to ensure Robo-teacher learns from a diverse set of exemplars to ensure that it does not later exhibit biased actions that may be localised to a specific area or region.

Undoubtedly, much room for algorithmic optimisation exists in this scenario, but I will leave that for a much more technically oriented paper to explore. Suffice it to say that learning behaviour through observation or data is a field of computer science that is increasingly gaining traction and for which many proofs of the concept exist (van Lent and Laird 2001; Argall et al. 2009; Brys et al. 2015; Howard and Muntean 2016; Duan et al. 2017). Once Robo-teacher has learned from all the identified exemplar teachers, it stores this information inside its internal knowledge database.

Only learning what others have done in various scenarios does not necessarily mean that Robo-teacher will make the right decision in a given situation. For that, it will need to have a mechanism that allows it to make a moral choice in a given scenario in real-time. For this to happen, Robo-teacher will likely need much of the same sensors that were used to capture information used to observe the exemplar teachers. The sensor data and the learned system of moral values could be employed by a decision procedure that will allow it to make ethical choices.

---

[6]Incidentally, picking a specific and constrained context also helps minimise the burden of the framing problem in AI (Mayo 2003). The latest research suggests that this problem is solvable by grounding semantics in multiple perceptual modalities (Kiela 2017).

There are many decision procedures in computer science, many of which are centred around probability and utility theory (Russell and Norvig 2009). These include probabilistic reasoning, decision networks, utility functions and Markov decision processes, amongst many others. I refer the reader to the works of Peterson (2009), Russell and Norvig (2009), and Conitzer et al. (2017) for a more detailed discussion of the topic.

In this case, a probabilistic approach such as a Markov decision process (MDP) could be appropriate, especially if all the morally relevant information can be measured through sensors. If we assume that some potentially relevant data, such as anger and frustration, cannot be measured or modelled by the sensors, then a partially observable Markov decision process (POMDP) could be employed, as suggested by Abel et al. (2016). Of course, the choice of the relevant decision procedure will ultimately lie with the designers.

The effectiveness of the decision procedure will depend on how well it is implemented. Even if it is implemented moderately well, this will allow Robo-teacher to make some moral decisions in real-time. This will also enable it to have a balance (i.e. golden mean) between merely doing what it has learned from exemplar teachers, and reacting to specific situations in real-time.

Once Robo-teacher has identified exemplar teachers and learned from their behaviour, and is equipped with a decision-theocratic procedure, it is now ready to go back to the classroom and hopefully handle situations where Nancy is disruptive in a better way. A myriad of options for handling the situation exist, such as speaking to Nancy directly, ordering her to leave the classroom, making her sit by herself in a corner, barring her from asking any further questions, reporting her or even merely ignoring her (Levinson and Fay 2016). All these choices, and undoubtedly many others, exist, and they will all have different consequences. Clearly, having the benefit of "knowing" what others have done in similar situations will prove to be useful in this scenario.

Once Robo-teacher has chosen an action, it will need to look out for feedback regarding the effect (either from the learner(s), teachers or parents), and to further learn from it so that it can handle the situation better in future. Though the emphasis of exemplarism is on learning from the examples of others, there is nothing stopping Robo-teacher from learning from its own examples, whether good or bad.

As has been seen in this scenario, how exemplarism will work itself out in practice is highly dependent on the scenario or context where it is implemented. Many of the choices and assumptions I made in this scenario were centred around ensuring that the AMA could identify moral exemplars, represent the classroom world computationally and use a suitable decision-theocratic approach to make moral decisions. Undoubtedly, different choices and assumptions could be made. Still, ultimately, all of them have to contend with the fact that we are dealing with computationally rational AMAs with weak machine ethics.

What this scenario has hopefully shown is that exemplarism can be practically implemented in a specific context. Even though this scenario was in a classroom context, a similar one could be derived to show how it might work in a myriad of other contexts. I do not doubt that a lot of technical challenges are there. Still, I hope this has shown that it is possible to make choices that minimise the technical burden without compromising on the chosen ethical theory. In this scenario, the AMA still had to select moral exemplars, learn from them and finally make moral choices in real-time.

6 Anticipated Challenges in the Design of Exemplarist Artificial Moral Agents

Even though the scenario above hinted at possible ways to overcome some of the challenges inherent in building AMAs with exemplarism, nevertheless it is still necessary to note these challenges because they likely cannot be universally solved. Each solution to a challenge will depend on the scenario and context.

The Challenge of Identifying Moral Exemplars Likely the most significant criticism of exemplarism has to do with the issue of identifying moral exemplars (Szutta 2019). In Zagzebski's theory, people use the *emotion* of admiration to identify moral exemplars. This *emotion* is subject to education over time through observation of the emotional responses that others have, or had, towards a specific moral exemplar.

The challenge, however, is that emotions can be quite unreliable as a method for determining moral exemplars. They certainly cannot be used in weak machine ethics AMAs to identify them either. Even though Zagzebski (2010) argues that exemplarism is not grounded in virtues, Szutta (2019) counters this by stating that people will likely still need some prior knowledge of virtues which will help them identify moral exemplars.

I have already argued in Section 4.2 that it is possible to identify exemplars without a descriptive understanding of virtues, in both human beings and AMAs. Szutta's counter has mostly to do with the practicality of identifying moral exemplars, especially if the emotion of admiration is unreliable (Szutta 2019). What is important for this article is to demonstrate possible ways in which AMAs can practically identify moral exemplars.

So what could be some of the practical ways in which an AMA might feasibly identify moral exemplars? Would the AMA need to engage with other moral agents? Would it read local news stories about local heroes? Would it observe the moral behaviour of other agents in relevant environments? The answers to these questions can affect what, and how quickly, the AMA learns! These limitations may force a departure from strict adherence to Zagzebski's theory when building the AMA.

For instance, it may be possible to look at various other metrics for identifying moral exemplars, as opposed to depending on the emotion of admiration. It may also mean that the AMA should be given pre-selected moral exemplars to learn from. For instance, if the AMA is a healthcare robot, then it could be given pre-selected heroes in the industry to learn from.

I liken this to raising a child, where the parents might initially keep the child in specifically defined spaces, and given specific material to learn from. Over time, parents will start allowing the child more freedom to explore as they grow older.

Perhaps a similar approach to that may be required when "raising" the AMA, where we might start with well-defined environments and exemplars, and allow the agent more latitude to explore as we mature the technology for building AMAs.

In the scenario discussed in the previous section, I had to make the assumption that a database of moral exemplars, complete with a numeric indicator of how well they performed, was available in order to allow the AMA to choose them without active assistance independently. Similar workarounds like this will be needed to allow AMAs to identify moral exemplars absent from the emotion of admiration.

The Challenge of Learning Moral Behaviour from Moral Exemplars Learning moral behaviour through observation is less of a challenge for human beings because we likely have built-in capacities that allow us to formulate and assimilate the moral values of our social context (Churchland 2014). However, emulating this capability in computationally based AMAs with weak machine ethics is not straightforward. Firstly, the AMA has no such built-in capacity to pick up moral cues through observation and use these to formulate a moral value system. We have to resort to the familiar method in machine learning systems of engineering features that the AMA can "look" out for. As Howard and Muntean (2016) discovered in their quest to build an AMA, moral values are very abstract, and therefore not easily translatable into a computational framework.

A related challenge has to do with the quantity and diversity of data that can be collected for learning purposes. Even if we managed to engineer moral features that the AMA could observe, we would still have to deal with the challenge of collecting enough data for the machine learning process. We would also need to ensure that we have enough data points for the AMA to learn a general representation of moral values, and not to replicate the behaviour of a single or few moral exemplars. In other words, the AMA needs to have both sufficient and generalised data available to formulate an internal representation of moral values.

In the scenario that I discussed in the previous section, I described a classroom environment wherein Robo-teacher had access to a wide array of data from which to learn. In different scenarios, pre-selected and stored data may not be readily available for the AMA to learn from, and alternative methods (such as learning through direct observation or direct feedback from human beings) may need to be employed. In the end, designers have to figure out how the data for training exemplarist AMAs will be sourced, and how the AMA will be trained. What the scenario showed is that carefully planning how the data for training AMAs will be sourced, and storing such data ahead of time, can significantly simplify the task of training the AMA.

I believe the challenges above point to the inescapable reality that building exemplarism into AMAs that function in general contexts is likely not possible with current technology. However, should the context and scenario be constrained and well defined, with data available before deployment and in real-time, then I believe the prospect of building an exemplarist AMA using currently available technology is possible.

7 Conclusion

My main reason for suggesting that exemplarism be used to build AMAs is that it can assist in making them meet community expectations of moral value, especially in highly specific contexts. As shown in the scenario discussed earlier, Robo-teacher will likely learn how to deal with classroom ethics in a manner that is aligned with how other teachers in the school or district would expect. This is a key feature of exemplarism, and I suggest that it can be used to build AMAs in many different contexts.

There are definite challenges to building exemplarist AMAs, mostly to do with finding computationally feasible ways to identify and learn from moral exemplars absent of the built-in capacities that make these tasks relatively simple for human moral agents. Despite these challenges, I believe careful planning and selection of an appropriate context, with the relevant data available, can make the task of building an exemplarist AMA possible using currently available technology.

I believe intensified research into the automated identification of moral exemplars, and the ability to automatically record, tag, store and learn from morally relevant data, is required to progress the exemplarist AMA project beyond the constraints that currently hold it back. I believe when these constraints are solved in a technically feasible manner, then artificial agents and society can co-exist without having to incur the risks of loss of human control and agency. Until then, I suggest we must begin experimental designs and deployments of exemplarist AMAs in contexts where the technical constraints can be circumvented.

References

Abel, D., MacGlashan, J., Littman, M.L. (2016). Reinforcement learning as a framework for ethical decision making. In *AAAI workshop - technical report*, (Vol. WS-16-01 pp. 54–61). www.aaai.org.

Abney, K. (2012). Robotics, ethical theory, and metaethics: a guide for the perplexed. In Lin, P., Abney, K., Bekey, G. (Eds.) *Robot Ethics, the ethical and social implications of robotics*, (Vol. 3 pp. 35-52): The MIT Press, chap.

Aghion, P.J., Benjamin, F., Jones, C.I. (2017). Artificial intelligence and economic growth. Tech. rep., National Bureau of Economic Research.

Allen, C., & Wallach, W. (2011). Moral machines: contradiction in terms, or abdication of human responsibility?. In Lin, P., Abney, K., Bekey, G.A. (Eds.) *Robot ethics* (p. 4): The MIT Press, chap.

Alzahrani, H. (2016). Artificial intelligence: uses and misuses. Global Journal of Computer Science and Technology 16(1s).

Anderson, M., & Anderson, S.L. (2007). Machine ethics: creating an ethical intelligent agent. *AI Magazine*, 28(4), 15. https://doi.org/10.1609/aimag.v28i4.2065 http://www.aaai.org/ojs/index.php/aimagazine/article/view/2065.

Anderson, S.L., & Anderson, M. (2011). A prima facie duty approach to machine ethics and its application to elder care. In *Workshops at the twenty-Fifth AAAI conference on artificial intelligence*.

Annas, J. (2011). *Intelligent virtue*. Oxford: Oxford University Press.

Argall, B.D., Chernova, S., Veloso, M., Browning, B. (2009). A survey of robot learning from demonstration. *Robotics and autonomous systems*, 57(5), 469–483.

Baum, S.D. (2017). Social choice ethics in artificial intelligence. AI and Society (October) 1–12, https://doi.org/10.1007/s00146-017-0760-1.

Brys, T., Harutyunyan, A., Suay, H.B., Chernova, S., Taylor, M.E., Nowé, A. (2015). Reinforcement learning from demonstration through shaping. In *Twenty-fourth international joint conference on artificial intelligence*.

Churchland, P.S. (2014). The neurobiological platform for moral values. *Behaviour*, *151*(2-3), 283–296.

Cloos, C. (2005). The utilibot project: an autonomous mobile robot based on utilitarianism. In *Machine ethics: papers from the 2005 AAAI fall symposium* (pp. 38–45). philpapers.org/archive/CLOTUP.2.pdf.

Conitzer, V., Sinnott-Armstrong, W., Borg, J.S., Deng, Y., Kramer, M. (2017). Moral decision making frameworks for artificial intelligence. In *ISAIM* (pp. 4831–4835). www.aaai.org.

Cowls, J., & Floridi, L. (2018). Prolegomena to a white paper on an ethical framework for a good AI society. SSRN Electronic Journal. https://doi.org/10.2139/ssrn.3198732. https://ssrn.com/abstract=3198732.

Dameski, A. (2018). A comprehensive ethical framework for AI entities : foundations. In Iklé, M., Franz, A., Rzepka, R., Goertzel, B. (Eds.) *International conference on artificial general intelligence, July* (pp. 42–51): Springer. https://doi.org/10.1007/978-3-319-97676-1.

Dignum, V. (2017). Responsible autonomy. In *Twenty-sixth International Joint Conference on Artificial Intelligence (IJCAI-17)*. https://doi.org/10.24963/ijcai.2017/655, arXiv:1706.02513.

Duan, Yan., Andrychowicz, Marcin., Stadie, Bradly., Jonathan, Ho., Open, AI., Schneider, Jonas., Sutskever, Ilya., Abbeel, Pieter., Zaremba, Wojciech. (2017). One-Shot Imitation Learning. In I. Guyon, U.V. Luxburg, S. Bengio, H. Wallach, R. Fergus, S. Vishwanathan, R. Garnett (Eds.) *Advances in Neural Information Processing Systems 30* (pp. 1087–1098): Curran Associates, Inc. http://papers.nips.cc/paper/6709-one-shot-imitation-learning.pdf.

Floridi, L., & Sanders, J.W. (2004). On the morality of artificial agents. *Minds and machines*, *14*(3), 349–379. https://doi.org/10.2139/ssrn.1124296.

Gershman, S.J., Horvitz, E.J., Tenenbaum, J.B. (2015). Computational rationality: a converging paradigm for intelligence in brains, minds, and machines. *Science*, *349*(6245), 273–278. https://doi.org/10.1126/science.aac6076. www.sciencemag.orgpapers2://publication/uuid/20A0106C-9CBA-472D-AAFB-69231964766F, arXiv:1011.1669v3.

Gips, J. (1995). Towards the ethical robot. In *Android epistemology* (pp. 243–252): MIT Press.

Himma, K.E. (2008). Artificial agency, consciousness, and the criteria for moral agency: what properties must an artificial agent have to be a moral agent? *Ethics and Information Technology*, *11*(1), 19–29. https://doi.org/10.1007/s10676-008-9167-5.

Horvitz, E.J. (1987). Reasoning about beliefs and actions under computational resource constraints. In *Proceedings of the third workshop on uncertainty in artificial intelligence, AAAI and Association for Uncertainty in Artificial Intelligence, July* (pp. 429–444). http://erichorvitz.com/u87.htm.

Howard, D., & Muntean, I. (2016). A minimalist model of the artificial autonomous moral agent (AAMA). In *AAAI Spring Symposium Series*.

Hursthouse, R., & Pettigrove, G. (2018). Virtue ethics. In Zalta, E. N. (Ed.) *The stanford encyclopedia of philosophy, winter 2018 edn*, Metaphysics Research Lab, Stanford University.

Johnson, D.G. (2006). Computer systems: moral entities but not moral agents. *Machine Ethics*, *9780521112*, 168–183. https://doi.org/10.1017/CBO9780511978036.012.

Kiela, D. (2017). Deep embodiment: grounding semantics in perceptual modalities. Tech. rep., University of Cambridge, Computer Laboratory. http://www.cl.cam.ac.uk/.

Kuipers, B. (2016). Human-like morality and ethics for robots.

van Lent, M., & Laird, J.E. (2001). Learning procedural knowledge through observation. In *K-CAP* (pp. 179–186), https://doi.org/10.1145/500737.500765.

Levinson, M., & Fay, J. (2016). *Dilemmas of educational ethics: cases and commentaries*. Cambridge: Harvard Education Press.

Liao, S.M. (2010). The basis of human moral status. *Journal of Moral Philosophy*, *7*(2), 1–31. https://doi.org/10.1163/174552409X12567397529106.

Mayo, M.J. (2003). Symbol grounding and its implications for artificial intelligence. In *Proceedings of the 26th Australasian computer science conference-Volume 16*, (Vol. 16 pp. 55–60). Darlinghurst: Australian Computer Society, Inc. http://portal.acm.org/citation.cfm?id=783106.783113&type=series.

Miller, F.D. (1984). Aristotle on rationality in action. *The Review of Metaphysics*, *37*(3), 499–520. https://www.jstor.org/stable/20128047.

Moor, J.H. (2006). The nature, importance, and difficulty of machine ethics. *IEEE intelligent systems*, *21*(4), 18–21.

Parthemore, J., & Whitby, B. (2013). What makes any agent a moral agent? Reflections on machine consciousness and moral agency. *International Journal of Machine Consciousness*, *5*(2), 105–129. https://pdfs.semanticscholar.org/3ff2/49fe3c8b3a2c94ae762b76b2dd0203f1f789.pdf.

Parthemore, J., & Whitby, B. (2014). Moral agency, moral responsibility, and artifacts: what existing artifacts fail to achieve (and why), and why they, nevertheless, can (and do!) make moral claims upon us. *International Journal of Machine Consciousness*, *6*(2), 141–161. https://doi.org/10.1142/S1793843014400162, http://www.worldscientific.com/doi/abs/10.1142/S1793843014400162.

Peterson, M. (2009). An introduction to decision theory. In *Cambridge introductions to philosophy*. Cambridge: Cambridge University Press, https://doi.org/10.1017/CBO9780511800917.

Pontier, M., & Hoorn, J. (2012). Toward machines that behave ethically better than humans do. In *Proceedings of the annual meeting of the cognitive science society*, Vol. 34.

Prasad, M. (2018). Social choice and the value alignment problem. In *Artificial intelligence safety and security* (pp. 291–314). London: Chapman and Hall/CRC.

Rottschaefer, W.A. (2000). Naturalizing ethics: the biology and psychology of moral agency. *Zygon®, 35*(2), 253–286.

Russell, S.J., & Norvig, P. (2009). *Artifical intelligence: a modern approach*, 3rd edn. Upper Saddle River: Prentice Hall. https://doi.org/10.1017/S0269888900007724. arXiv: 1707.02286, arXiv: 1011.1669v3.

Scheutz, M., & Malle, B.F. (2017). Moral robots. In Johnson, L.S.M., & Rommelfanger, K.S. (Eds.) *The Routledge handbook of neuroethics* (p. 24): Routledge, chap. https://doi.org/10.4324/9781315708652.ch24.

Simon, H.A. (1955). A behavioral model of rational choice. *The Quarterly Journal of Economics*, *69*(1), 99–118.

Slote, M. (1995). Agent-based virtue ethics. *Midwest Studies in Philosophy*, *20*(1), 83–101.

Sullins, J.P. (2006). When is a robot a moral agent? IRIE: International Review of Information Ethics http://sonoma-dspace.calstate.edu/handle/10211.1/427.

Szutta, N. (2019). Exemplarist moral theory–some pros and cons. *Journal of Moral Education*, *48*(3), 280–290. https://doi.org/10.1080/03057240.2019.1589435.

Torrance, S. (2008). Ethics and consciousness in artificial agents. *AI and Society*, *22*(4), 495–521. https://doi.org/10.1007/s00146-007-0091-8.

Vamplew, P., Dazeley, R., Foale, C., Firmin, S., Mummery, J. (2018). Human-aligned artificial intelligence is a multiobjective problem. *Ethics and Information Technology*, *20*(1), 27–40. https://doi.org/10.1007/s10676-017-9440-6.

Wallach, W., Franklin, S., Allen, C. (2010). A conceptual and computational model of moral decision making in human and artificial agents. *Topics in Cognitive Science*, *2*(3), 454–485. https://doi.org10.1111/j.1756-8765.2010.01095.x.

Zagzebski, L. (2010). Exemplarist virtue theory. *Metaphilosophy*, *41*(1-2), 41–57. https://doi.org/10.1111/j.1467-9973.2009.01627.x.

Publisher's Note Springer Nature remains neutral with regard to jurisdictional claims in published maps and institutional affiliations.

Philosophy & Technology (2021) 34 (Suppl 1):S23–S44
https://doi.org/10.1007/s13347-020-00422-7

RESEARCH ARTICLE

In the Frame: the Language of AI

Helen Bones[1] • Susan Ford[2] • Rachel Hendery[1] • Kate Richards[1] •
Teresa Swist[1]

Received: 10 October 2019 / Accepted: 4 August 2020 / Published online: 20 August 2020
© Springer Nature B.V. 2020

Abstract
In this article, drawing upon a feminist epistemology, we examine the critical roles that philosophical standpoint, historical usage, gender, and language play in a knowledge arena which is increasingly opaque to the general public. Focussing on the language dimension in particular, in its historical and social dimensions, we explicate how some keywords in use across artificial intelligence (AI) discourses inform and misinform non-expert understandings of this area. The insights gained could help to imagine how AI technologies could be better conceptualised, explained, and governed, so that they are leveraged for social good.

Keywords Artificial intelligence · Machine learning · Social good · Language · Gender · Feminist epistemology · History · Linguistics · Framing · Cultural studies

1 Introduction

David Crystal (2015: 24) notes that, while everyone has some feeling for words, we are often so conflicted about their value that two diametrically opposed attitudes may exist in our minds at one and the same time:

Chapter 3 was originally published as Bones, H., Ford, S., Hendery, R., Richards, K. & Swist, T. Philosophy & Technology (2021) 34 (Suppl 1):S23–S44. https://doi.org/10.1007/s13347-020-00422-7.

✉ Rachel Hendery
r.hendery@westernsydney.edu.au

Helen Bones
h.bones@westernsydney.edu.au

Susan Ford
susan.ford@anu.edu.au

Kate Richards
kate.richards@westernsydney.edu.au

Teresa Swist
t.swist@westernsydney.edu.au

[1] Western Sydney University, Sydney, NSW, Australia

[2] Australian National University, Canberra, ACT, Australia

One is to see words as inadequate representations of thoughts, poor replacements for actions or a dangerous distraction from experiential realities. The other is to see them as indispensable for the expression of thoughts, a valuable alternative to actions, or a means of finding order in inchoate realities.

This paper argues that in both cases, language matters, just that in the first it is an impediment to understanding, and in the second it is crucial for it: language matters even when the person on the street thinks it does not. In a world where artificial intelligence (AI) is increasingly embedded in, even determining, our everyday lives, it is fundamental to democracy for citizens to be able to accurately interpret the particular words, phrases, metaphors, similes, and metonyms employed by practitioners, journalists, and citizens when they talk about artificial intelligence (AI), machine learning (ML), and "deep learning". Only with accurate understanding of such concepts can we choose when to accept the outputs of AI algorithms and when to question them; when to implement processes based on AI and when to forgo them; or even to imagine what problems might be amenable to AI-based solutions and which are not, or not yet.

Specifically, without a democratic approach, it is difficult to leverage AI for social good. This is further complicated when there is no consensus about this concept of "social good". The "Artificial Intelligence (AI) for Social Good" (AI4SG) literature at least describes the term in the form of a research theme which "aims to use and advance artificial intelligence to address societal issues and improve the wellbeing of the world"—which is being applied across the domains of agriculture, education, environmental sustainability, healthcare, combating information manipulation, social care and urban planning, public safety, and transportation (Shi, Wang & Fang, 2020). Going directly to the practical achievement of social good, Floridi, Cowls, King and Taddeo (2020: 3) propose that, given the variability of AI4SG applications and outcomes, identifying factors "that are *particularly relevant* to AI as a technology designed and used for the *advancement of social good*" is a way to "avoid unnecessary failures and accidental successes". On the other hand, Binns (2018) addresses the theoretical side of the question—how can an AI programme (or program) be assessed as ethical or not? He relies on the existing notion of "public reason" developed by political philosophers and defined by Quong (2013) as the requirement that "Our laws and political institutions must be justifiable to each of us by reference to some common point of view, despite our deep differences and disagreements", to tease out how the democratising of AI, in the form of "algorithmic accountability", could be made to happen. Accountability "involves the provision of reasons, explanations and justifications" (2019: 547); algorithmic accountability therefore involves tying AI algorithms via those facets of accountability to the agreed norms and standards which operate within a society—according at least to a "democratic political ideal" (2019: 548). Our argument begins at an even more basic point than Binns': AI already surrounds us and is discussed, but the discussion is on the wrong track so language is the first thing which must be addressed. Our position is that, whatever else is needed, there cannot even begin to be any guarantee of AI for social good without a democratic discourse.

We note that even in professions such as medicine, where AI abounds, individual doctors are not likely to have a deep technical understanding of the algorithms that underlie these approaches and may accept its benefits or be impressed with imagined possibilities on the basis of the surrounding discourse (Buch et al. 2018 is an example of this). Similarly, the impact of powerful language around AI can be seen when development environments are marketed to groups such as digital agencies and financial institutions. The "Robodebt" roll out by the Australian federal government involving automatic data matching across agencies is an example of this as it leveraged respondents' fears and ignorance of the processes.[1]

Philosophers and others have raised concerns about the dangers AI poses to freedom of speech, and individual liberty and autonomy if we are unable to engage in debate about its realities. And we are not able to, as long as all those engaging in such debate do not clearly understand what AI really is or how it works.[2] Didier et al. (2015) sound the alarm in no uncertain terms, noting that some AI practitioners imply:

> that we are all engaged in a common endeavor, when in fact AI is dominated by a relative handful of mostly male, mostly white and east Asian, mostly young, mostly affluent, highly educated technoscientists and entrepreneurs and their affluent customers. A majority of humanity is on the outside looking in, and it is past time for those working on AI to be frank about it.

Leaving development and full understanding of AI (and digital technology more broadly) in the hands of such a small segment of society means that technical jargon, metaphors, analogy, and linguistic shorthand that may be meaningful to this small group risks being utterly opaque, or worse, misleading, when heard or used by those outside the circle. The narrowness of the demographics of this inner circle, moreover, means that rich sources of potentially clearer, more accurate, or more widely accessible metaphors and terminology remain unplumbed. As two very simple examples from computing more broadly (via Haviland et al. 2013: 379), the metaphor of a computer "crashing" was found to be obscure to some speakers of Fulah, who do not have cars, and was replaced by a term that literally refers to a cow falling over. Similarly, in Zapotec, a language spoken by people who do not have windows in their houses, the desktop metaphor of "windows" had to be replaced by the word for "eyes". This use of more culturally salient terms would never have been imagined were it not for Fulah and Zapotec speaking programmers. Feminist standpoint theory in fact argues that more even than diversity of worldviews, we would benefit from *centering* minority or marginalised perspectives, as this helps expose the particularly problematic parts of the status quo (D'Ignazio and Klein 2019: chapter 4, referring specifically to the design of computational systems).

Overall, how language permeates and shapes the priorities of research, policy and legislation, programming, plus the broader workforce, demands much further attention be focussed upon the different discourses and practices of AI4SG. For instance, which

---

[1] Australian Broadcasting Corporation (ABC) reporting throughout 2019 struggled to express clearly and succinctly what rules are being applied; and this is part of the problem, as it is hard to determine whether there is an AI process involved. A senior partner in the law firm managing the class action to challenge the legality of the Robodebt policy states that "to simply collect money from hundreds of thousands of people by the simplistic application of an imperfect computer algorithm is wrong." (ABC News 2019).

[2] Succinctly put by Didier et al. in *Science*, in response to a set of articles published in the same journal: "Given the grievous shortcomings of national governance and the even weaker capacities of the international system, it is dangerous to invest heavily in AI without political processes in place that allow those who support and oppose the technology to engage in a fair debate." (Didier et al. 2015: 1064); on the dangers for medicine see e.g. Cabitza et al. (2017); see also Challen et al. (2019).

discourses and practices are privileged, or marginalised, by whom, how—and to what effect. For example, Collett and Dillon (2019) highlight that the most significant challenges to gender equality presented by AI developments include: bridging gender theory and AI practice, law and policy, biased datasets, and diversity in the AI workforce. To address these issues, they call for further research focussed upon diversification of the workforce, data-set guidelines and narratives, how emerging legislation and policy will impact gender equality, and the need for interdisciplinary and cross-sectoral collaborations.

None of the writers of the present paper is a philosopher or an AI professional, but we have felt the same need to intervene in what at present seems a juggernaut of "AI speak"—a tendency we noticed even while we were jointly engaged on a course to learn about AI. What we found ubiquitous in the presentation of AI concepts (both within the particular Massive Online Open Course (MOOC) and within the further readings some of us were doing) was a set of terms based on metaphors of human capacities without, it seemed to us, sufficient justification.[3] The set of terms in current use is open to critique not only for its ethical dangers but for its opaqueness. We are inspired to pick up the powerful critique of the AI programme offered by Powles and Nissenbaum, who point to language evincing "problematic self-righteousness" and the self-justification practices by which "recognizing and acknowledging bias can be seen as a *strategic concession*" (Powles and Nissenbaum 2018). We wish to demonstrate some of the language-related causes of these problems in AI as currently practised and experienced.

In doing so, we employ three main methods, which we interweave through case studies of some key terminology. The first of our methods is a historical approach, which highlights some of the broad trends which have characterised the field and the ways in which discourse informs practice. Trends, particularly in software technologies, conspicuously drive the discourse and make it challenging to arrive at a proper historical analysis for recent history, and to see which, if any, internally motivated trend could lead to ethical AI. To cut across this difficulty, Steels (2007) advocates a "design stance" which involves "investigating in principle by what mechanisms intelligence is achieved" (18); Steels also wants a future AI programme to "not pretend to be modeling the human brain or human intelligence" (28). Progressing AI for social good therefore requires novel ways of exploring not only who benefits and is in control, but also the related question of how knowledge is rendered intelligible.

The second part of our method, therefore, applying a feminist lens, allows us to explore how values, language, and norms are produced—and to contest reductive approaches to AI. For example, in her article "Artificial Intelligence and Women's Knowledge. What Can Feminist Epistemologies Tell Us", Alison Adam (1995) argues that "the success or failure of AI is a cultural question" (407). Adam's view is that traditional epistemological assumptions of AI focus too narrowly on the modelling of intelligent human behaviour and ignore power relations in wider society. This is an epistemology which relies on knowledge (or *knowing that*) deemed universal, disembodied, and separate from the observer.[4] In contrast, Adam proposes a feminist

---

[3] We note that some recent presentations such as a Finnish online AI course make the point that "words can be misleading" quite explicitly (Roos 2019).

[4] For quick illustration, this kind of thinking appears in one of the early histories of modern computing, where the author, an engineer turned historian, refers to Rene Descartes' "discovery" of analytical geometry (rather than e.g. "invention") (Goldstine 1993: 13).

epistemology which asks "*how* AI systems are used to represent knowledge, what *kind* of knowledge and *whose* knowledge they contain." (407; emphasis added)—an approach which recognises a plurality of views (*knowing how*) based on knowledge emerging from particular and situated skills. Berendt (2019) describes the powerful role of "framing": how frames inform problem definitions and methods—and are in turn are reinforced by AI applications.

The third lens through which our paper considers these terms is linguistic. Terminology matters. At the very least, the selection of word stems, source languages, and figures of speech to describe new technologies encodes a culturally specific viewpoint. At the far extreme, there is the strong version of the Sapir-Whorf hypothesis, in which the language we speak actually determines the way we think. To some extent, this is indisputable: children who grow up in a language where absolute directions (e.g. North, South, East, West) must be specified on a noun for the sentence to be grammatical do pay more attention to these compass directions as they move through the world (Levinson 1997). A recent study of Swedish speakers found that a decade after a gender-non-specific third person pronoun became part of the everyday language, speakers are less likely to assume male gender of ambiguous cartoon characters (Lindqvist et al. 2019). Because of this potential for the terminology we use to influence the way we think, it is worth considering how new terminology arises, what connotations a word or idiom carries with it, and how and when we can influence these processes.

We would argue that consideration of the language of AI is a very timely matter. When a community discovers or imports a new technology, whether that be the wheel, farming, motorcars, computers, or artificial intelligence, new terminology also becomes necessary. At an early stage, there may be multiple competing neologisms or adaptations/expansions of terminology that eventually resolve into a common consensus (consider e.g. "text-message", "message", "SMS", or "text"). In the case of AI, we would argue that society is right on the cusp of this consensus stage. The words and phrases we use to describe AI algorithms and related concepts have started to infiltrate everyday speech and people are becoming comfortable with accepted terminology. If we want to reconsider the language and figures of speech used in this space, the time to do so is now. We can discover gaps between how computing professionals communicate and how the general public understands the terminology by examining the use of particular terms by each.

In the following subsections, we will therefore take some of these terms ("data", "memory", "brain", and "learning") and consider them in their historical and cultural dimensions, alongside the often problematic ways they frame the discourse of AI, in particular for people who may be affected by or even applying AI, without necessarily having complete understanding of the underlying algorithms. We examine how these terms have been used in the history of computing, alongside how they are understood by those who are not necessarily computing professionals. For the latter, we examine which other terms frequently appear together with our terms of interest (i.e. their "collocations" or "collocates" in a corpus linguistic approach). For this, we use three corpora: the Corpus of Global Web-Based English (GloWBE), an international corpus of English collected from the web between 2012 and 2013, containing 1.9 billion words (Davies 2013); the British National Corpus (BNC), a 100-million-word corpus of written and spoken English from the 1980s–1990s, which while limited to UK English includes many more pre- and non-digital sources (Davies 2004); and the *Time Magazine Corpus* (Davies 2007) to see how collocations have changed over time.

In the next section, we turn to an overview of how technology, knowledge, and gender reinforce values and embed norms—via a range of cultural habits, societal patterns, conversations, and voices. Building on the importance of "framing" which we introduce in this section, we then examine each of our case study terms in detail, from a historical, socio-cultural, and linguistic perspective. Our final example is a more drawn-out application of this approach to the example of machine learning, considering whether and in what ways it maps to a general understanding of the word "learning". We conclude with a discussion of the practical implications of these critiques and what the steps towards change should be.

2 Technology, Knowledge, and Gender

Feminist theories of knowledge provide both motive and means to reconfigure AI: women suffer from its present extreme bias (e.g. Caliskan et al. 2017; Leavy 2018) and gender theory provides the means to see where to intervene to improve equity in the applications of AI. Gender, race, and power in AI "affects how AI companies work, what products get built, who they are designed to serve, and who benefits from their development" (West et al. 2019: 5). Understanding the relationship between technology, knowledge, and gender can help identify how such "discriminating systems" (5) propagate themselves over time and become entrenched framings across society. These concerns hold likewise for other dimensions of structural power such as race, socio-economic status, and Western bias, among others, and the intersection of these (Buolamwini and Gebru 2018). While we are focussing in this paper on gender, we conceive of this in an intersectional framework where other dimensions of inequality mean that gender effects play out very differently for different demographics.

It is well established that there is a perceived link between technical competence and masculinity (Lie 1995; Abbiss 2011; Pechtelidis et al. 2015) and that this manifests already from an early age (Margolis and Fisher 2002: 22). These early biases, reinforced in manifold ways throughout society and over time, can determine lives and career paths. Representations of women in STEM-related fields depend on "gendered discourses which associate the production of knowledge/science/the intellect/the public sphere with masculinity and communication/caring/the body/the private sphere with femininity" (Mendick and Moreau 2013: 329). Women are therefore less likely to participate in technological fields because of internalised ideas about it not being naturally suited to them (326).

The ability to use key technologies of the day, and involvement in the creation of such technologies, is intertwined with power, which is a self-perpetuating system that privileges the already-powerful. As Nathan Ensmenger points out, "who has the power to set certain technical and economic priorities are fundamentally social considerations that deeply influence the technological development process" (Ensmenger 2004: 96). Sometimes this power can be deliberately wielded to privilege certain groups. According to Ruth Oldenziel, the association of technology with masculinity was a twentieth-century invention in response to women's increasing presence in the public sphere (Oldenziel 1999: 10). This ties in with Marie Hicks's (2017) argument which centres around the displacement of a largely female workforce in the early days of British computing as the field became more desirable into the 1960s and beyond. According to Hicks, Britain's "computerization [was] an explicitly hegemonic project built on labor categories designed to perpetuate particular forms of class status" and a part of "a deliberate government policy to reinforce gender roles" (6).

As Margolis and Fisher ask, "Why should it matter if the inventors, designers, and creators of computer technology are mostly male?" (2002: 3). The answer is much more serious than women merely missing out on exciting careers and economic opportunities. The "near absence of women's voices at the drawing board" means that the systems that increasingly underpin society are "built around male cultural models" (3). A very concrete example is early voice recognition systems that were calibrated to male voices, with the consequence that "women's voices were literally unheard".

Even critiques of AI are susceptible to gendered power imbalances. Ellen Broad (2019) fears that these biases are creeping into the field of AI ethics, which was originally dominated by women. Now it is becoming more mainstream, however, the discussions are increasingly male-dominated:

> What troubles me is that what 'ethical AI' encompasses often seems to end up in these conversations being redefined as a narrow set of technical approaches that can be applied to existing, male-dominated professions. Even as the women in these professions – and many of the influential women I just cited are computer scientists and machine-learning researchers – are doing pathbreaking work on the limitations (as well as the strengths) of technical methods quantifying bias and articulating notions of 'fairness', these technical interpretations of ethics become the sole lens through which 'ethical AI' is commoditised. Ethical AI is thus recast as a 'new', previously unconsidered technical problem to be solved, and solved by men (78).

Diversity and gender theory in the development of machine learning technologies, Leavy (2018:14) argues, can improve training data, and support fairness in algorithms, as well as help assess the "potential impact of gender bias in the context of the intended use of the technology". These and other socio-technical solutions to this problem have been a focus of interest in recent AI for Good literature, for example Madras et al. (2019) and Mitchell et al. (2019). It is of course still no easy matter because there are multiple sites where inequity occurs. As one way of intervening, we propose that a feminist lens can interrupt and disrupt dominant *framings* of AI. This approach helps to reveal the complexity and diversity of technical language: how it is always situated and evolves with culture and practice and why its critique is key to change for social good.

3 Terminology Case Studies

In this section, we take up this challenge of critiquing framings of AI, by examining in turn some key phrases from the discourse around AI, in their historical, socio-cultural, and linguistic specifics.

Reprinted from the journal

3.1 "Data"

The term "data" is first attested in the seventeenth century, originally in a more restricted sense as facts underlying mathematical calculations (for example "Data for such triangles as have been Constructed generally, the vertical angle being supposed obtuse or acute" (Leybourn 1802: 1). Since the late twentieth century, it has been used to mean numerical information more broadly. Its use for information stored or transmitted by computers dates to the early days of computing in the mid-twentieth century. There are a few such examples already in the *Time Magazine Corpus* from the 1940s. Exploring more recent collocations for the term in the GloWbE, we find that people conceive of data as something that exists independent of human creation or intervention. We *collect*, *obtain*, *store*, or *report* it. These words appear in collocation with data with frequencies of 5674, 1475, 604, and 932 times per million words respectively, which can be compared with the frequencies of the less common collocates discussed later. It changes hands because we *provide* or *release* it to others. We then *store* it, or we *analyze* it. We *base* things on it. More actively, it *supports* things, *shows* things, or *indicates* things. These are all verb collocates in the top 100 most frequent in the GloWbE (most in the top 50). The verbs that suggest a conception of data as a human artefact are much less frequent: *control* appears as the 281st most common collocate, 154 times per million words; *designed* only appears 234 times per million words; *manipulated* 138 times. Some collocates at least indicate an awareness that data must be *interpreted* (274 times per million), *linked* (145), or *examined* (401).

This conception of data as objects that exist in the world independent of humans is in line with the prevalent model of data as something that can always be owned or controlled. If data are objective items that people can collect, then they can be stored, given, and received, just like any other thing that people might take from the world around us: plant samples, for example, or sand from a beach. This perception feeds into the "black box" attitude to AI, in which the dataset on which a model is trained remains hidden, usually because it might be considered a commercial product.

One reframing that has been proposed in the humanities literature is data as "capta". This was first proposed by Russo (1957) but has reached popularity through Johanna Drucker's engagement with and expansion of this idea (2010, 2011). The idea behind this reframing is that "[d]ifferences in the etymological roots of the terms data and capta make the distinction between constructivist and realist approaches clear. Capta is 'taken' actively while data is assumed to be a 'given' able to be recorded and observed." (Drucker 2011). Drucker goes on to argue that data are "constructed as an interpretation of the phenomenal world, not inherent in it" and that "all data is capta".

We suggest rather that there is a continuum of data along which capta is a more useful term for items towards one end of the continuum than the other. At the end for which the term is less useful, we have information that is simple, objective, and only read or handled by machines, to be transmitted to other machines, with minimal transformation of its form. For example, the status of a machine as connected to power or disconnected might set a bit to 0 or 1 and that might be read by another machine, which might write this information onto its hard drive. The subsequent list of on/off transitions stored by the second machine was provided to it directly by the first machine. There is no risk in using a term like "data" for this kind of information. It becomes more complex if the information from the first machine is stored in a database, because the structure of that database is designed by humans. Even adding timestamps brings in a subjective classification system that relies on human decision-making: what format is used; to what degree of precision; is it stored as an array of characters, a decimal value, an integer, or a datetime datatype? Such decisions carry inherent assumptions about what kinds of queries a person is likely to make of the database and for what purpose. Nevertheless, it is still relatively low risk to conceptualise these kinds of data as *given* not *taken*, and to elide the human element involved.

At the far other end of the continuum, however, there are very personal, qualitative, subjective data, for which the term *capta* is an important reminder of the interpretive nature of this information. These might include, for example, biometric data captured by fitness trackers, analysed for health indicators, and stored by an insurance company. Even at the first step of data collection, the bits and bytes stored reflect human decision-making (the hardware in the device, how it is calibrated, how it is worn, whether it is instead attached to the person's pet in order to falsely inflate the amount of movement) and at each subsequent processing step the data undergo filtering, classification, and cleaning based on human assumptions and decisions.

Returning to the issue at hand, public perception of AI, the data fed into AI algorithms frequently sit towards the end of the continuum for which it is important to conceive them as capta. Even for photo classification, for example, where the image is converted into a list of bits representing the colours of each pixel, this is not straightforward objective information "given" to the algorithm from the world. The lens of the camera, the human decisions that went into selecting the subject, framing it, and choosing camera settings, and any subsequent image processing all underlie and determine that sequence of bits. Lorna Roth (2013) shows how early decisions made about chemical processing of film incorporated racial bias that has had long-lasting effects on photographic technology to this day.

In reframing "data" to "capta" and thus emphasising its nature as a series of decisions made by humans, it also becomes more apparent that usual capitalist practices around ownership, storage and transferral of ownership cannot or should not always straightforwardly map onto our data behaviours. Concerns in recent decades about *data sovereignty* (see e.g. Kukutai and Taylor 2016) have taken up this critique of data as something that can or should be commercialisable, taken or given, and rather have considered it as something intrinsically bound to the people from whom it is derived (see also, for example, the EU approach to data protection, which also considers personal data as a part of personal autonomy). Data sovereignty and approaches like that of the EU are primarily concerned with personal data—data about a person, about things intrinsically bound to a person's identity (e.g. ICIP), and data created by a person. Reframing data as capta, however, helps us to see the personal layers in even supposedly more objective datasets and to consider whether commoditization of these too is problematic: if a dataset is not about people but it is shaped by peoples' decisions at various levels (hardware for capturing it, software for storing it, subsequent cleaning, processing, and analysis), who does it belong to, and who should make subsequent decisions about its usage? Conceptualising data/capta as a series of decisions that create relationships among people, and between people and the world, instead of as objects, can help us imagine new models for interaction with this data/capta.[5]

3.2 "Memory", "Brain"

Similarly to how we proceeded in the previous section, a historical consideration of the terms "memory",[6] "reading"/"writing", and "brain" helps us understand some of the issues with their current-day usage. While this discussion considers computers more generally, the common conception of the computer is foundational to a public understanding of AI, and the equation of a neural net with a kind of artificial brain makes the brain a particularly important source of analogy to investigate in the current context. These terms have been in use since the beginning of modern computing—the "memory" and "reading" metaphors (referring to electronic storage and transfer) obviously draw on the semantic domain of human faculties to describe the structure of computer hardware and software: that is, they *map* the primary semantic domain of computing to the secondary domain of human ability in order to explain the former. And the word "brain" to denote the computer itself does not merely map, it asserts. Even today, explanations of computing for beginners frequently rely on this "brain" analogy (Wempen 2014: 38; Gookin 2013: 15, 37; Joos et al. 2019: 49, to give just a few examples).

In this example, understandings of the human body are adopted for understanding the machine, and in turn, understandings of the machine are applied to the human body. The semantics of the term "brain" and "memory" have become flavoured by both their biological and non-biological usages. Turkle (2005: 146ff) shows that even small children in recent times have begun to use computational metaphors to think about their own brain and body. She also discusses the use of such language in domains such as education ("debugging" 151), psychology ("mind as program" 222), and health (addiction as "hacking" or "programming" the brain 343).

The idea of the brain as a machine is not new to the digital age, of course. To investigate usage from before the age where the average speaker or writer was inspired by digital metaphors, we now turn to the British National Corpus (BNC, Davies 2004) rather than the GloWbE. While these data are limited to British English and may not apply more widely, this corpus consists of offline materials (newspapers, journals, books, fiction, letters, essays, meetings, radio shows, and informal conversations) from the 1980s and 1990s. The top 10 verbal collocates for brain in the BNC include "ticking", and indeed "the brain ticking over", and "a ticking brain" are common idioms derived from the literal ticking over of a clockwork machine. Other idioms applied to the brain from mechanical metaphors include "firing on all cylinders",

---

[5] This porous boundary between humans and data is also a key theme in the broader history of computing through the rise of the concept of "user experience design" (UX), from Joint Application Development (Wood and Silver 1995; see also Sumner 2014: 310–311), through to user-centred design (Okolloh 2009), and finally a web 2.0 model whereby end-users are now *themselves used* as cogs in the machine, whose value is in the marketability of their data and the predictability of their behaviour. The continued employment of the term *user* disguises this lack of agency and points to a disconnect between the understanding of computing professionals and the general public.

[6] For a brief period before the term "memory" became ubiquitous, a literal term "store" was used to refer to the main or immediate data store for a program.

"something clicking in one's brain", "engaging one's brain", "one's brain switching off", and the collocates "buzzing", "flashing", "slowing", and "conveyed", all of which occur frequently in the BNC. Some idioms and collocates, however, are specifically from the computing era, including the very phrase "does not compute" to mean "I do not understand". Neither is the conception of a machine as a kind of brain a new idea that is limited to AI or even computers. Zarkadakis (2015: part 1) traces our tendency to anthropomorphise inanimate objects back to the origins of humankind, in our need to understand the world around us as part of ourselves.

Historically, explanations of the new idea of computation frequently proceeded via a "brain" analogy; and although, as Sumner (2014: 328 n38) notes, "leading promoters of computing had objected to the 'brain' metaphor from the time of its creation", the general public embraced the terminology.[7] Edmund Berkeley, for example, wrote *Giant Brains, or Machines That Think* (1949) in order to explain the "new machines" to the general reader.[8] The main thesis is that it is both legitimate and necessary to call the new machines brains. But it is difficult not to see most of his arguments throughout the book as circular. Take for example an early passage (Berkeley 1949: 5):

> Now suppose we consider the basic operation of all thinking: in the human brain it is called learning and remembering and in a machine it is called storing information and then referring to it. For example, suppose you want to find 305 Main St Kalamazoo. You look up a map of Kalamazoo; the map is information kindly stored by other people for your use. When you study the map, notice the streets and the numbering, and then find where the house should be, you are thinking.
> A machine can do this. In the Bell Laboratories mechanical brain, for example [...]

He takes a real-life situation of wanting to find an address, characterises it as "thinking", describes it in information terms, and declares that a computer can do it. In presenting his material in this way, Berkeley is really only reproducing the reports of the wonders of "giant brains" and "mechanical brains" common in the press at the time.

Of a different order are two books, both influential, published in the 1950s which explored the 'memory' and 'brain' metaphors, albeit from different positions. B. V. Bowden's edited collection *Faster than Thought* provided a state of the art view of computing, at least in the UK, and especially directed towards its commercial development. John von Neumann's *The computer and the brain* (1958) was "an approach towards the understanding of the nervous system from the point of view of a mathematician" (1). Both discuss the implications of using "memory" and "brain" and other anthropomorphic/human-capacity words to refer to "automatic computing machinery".

---

[7] Sumner (2014: 327 n8&9) cites e.g. "An Electronic Brain", The Times, 1 November 1946, 2; "A New Electronic 'Brain': Britain Goes One Better", *Manchester Guardian*, 7 November 1946, 8. Perhaps one of the sources for the brain metaphor was the enormously popular novels of H. G. Wells, which frequently refer to the human brain and possible substitutes for, and extensions of, it.

[8] "I have tried to write this book so that it could be understood. I have attempted to explain machinery for computing and reasoning without using technical words any more than necessary." (Berkeley 1949: ix); Berkeley's interest in explanations for the general public is also reflected in his *A Guide to Mathematics for the Intelligent Nonmathematician* (1966).

In his introductory chapter of *Faster than Thought*, Bowden refers to both "storage" and "memory" ("The nucleus of all machines is the store or memory in which information can be kept. Several types of memory will be described later on" (1953: 28)); but he goes on to consider the import of the language he has used (emphasis added):

> At this point it is necessary to interpolate a remark to explain our apparent attribution to the machine of certain human qualities, such as *Memory, Judgment* and so on. Modern digital computers **are capable of** performing long and elaborate computations; **they can retain** numbers which have been presented to them or which **they themselves have derived** during the course of the computations; **they are, moreover, capable** of modifying their own programmes in the light of results which they have already derived. All these are operations which are usually performed (much more slowly and inaccurately) by human beings; but it is important to note that we do not claim that the machines can think for themselves. This is precisely what they cannot do. All the thinking has to be done for them in advance by the mathematician who planned their programme and they can do only what is demanded of them; even if he leaves the choice between two courses of action to be made by the machines, he instructs them in detail how to **make their choice** [...]
>
> These new machines have so many of the qualities of a human brain that one has to be rather careful if one is to avoid giving, by implication, a misleading impression. (Bowden 1953: 29)

Note here how often in these sentences agency is implicitly given to "the machines" by the use of active verbs with subject the machine (bolded phrases): Though the human programmer may "instruct them in detail" the machines still "make their choice". In the terminology of Speech Act theory (Austin 1962), the description of how a computer works in the first paragraph of this passage has the perlocutionary force of presenting computers as independent agents by virtue of this agency—the words have a rhetorical effect beyond that necessarily intended by the writer. The writer Bowden has misgivings about this effect but cannot countermand it so long as this terminology is all that is available to him.

Meanwhile in the USA, the most important thinker after Alan Turing about mind and machine among the practitioners[9] was John von Neumann. Before the war, von Neumann had made significant contributions to mathematics but from 1943 to 19244, his interests turned strongly to the new machines (Aspray 1990: 25–48). Von Neumann's *The computer and the brain* (1958) was developed as a "comparison" (39) of computers and the brain: description of each occupying roughly equal parts of the book.[10] Since his explicit purpose is to make that comparison the author does *not* call computers "brains", rather, he calls them "[large electronic] computing machines"

---

[9] The term "practitioners" is used loosely to refer to those with practical interest in computers and theorising from that interest, as opposed to Gilbert Ryle for example.

[10] Von Neumann remarks on the lack of a theory of computers, which at this point he generalises as "automata" (1958: 2).

(2, 3 etc.; "machine" 5, 6, etc.). In the second half of the book, the author identifies several "components", as he calls them, of the human brain and nervous system so that he can compare them severally to the components of computing machines (39). This seems reasonable and interesting, but then there comes a passage rather startling in its implications (60, emphasis added):

> The discussions up to this point have not taken into account a component whose presence in the nervous system is highly plausible, if not certain - **if for no other reason than that it has played a vital role in all artificial computing machines constructed to date**, and its significance is, therefore, probably a matter of principle, rather than of accident. I mean the *memory*. I will therefore turn now to the discussion of this component, or rather subassembly, of the nervous system.

The phrase in boldface shows that at this point in his argument von Neumann feels that his part-by-part comparison has demonstrated not that we can build machines which imitate human brains (that would be the too-easy part) but that we do not even need to—the human brain is already (as it were) a machine; i.e. if simple equivalence has been demonstrated, the rest follows.

In this passage the author has deployed terminology relevant to his rhetorical purpose to offer the startling conclusion that *because* a "memory" had been found necessary in the architecture of computers, it must therefore exist in the human brain; in other words, he takes the then state of computing machinery (the date of writing was 1956) to be a reliable guide to at least part of the capacity of the human brain.[11] The point is driven home by the immediate switch to the terminology which von Neumann feels he has now justified: "this component, or rather subassembly, of the nervous system".

This brief analytical sketch of the descriptive language used in the immediate postwar first period of modern computing by three influential writers, Berkeley, Bowden, and von Neumann, begins to trace how certain modes of describing began. It shows how the language appropriate to description of computers was still in development and under negotiation, but already displaying a tendency to use anthropomorphic terms. The present-day result of this is that people's understanding of how computers work is flavoured by their understanding of the human brain, and their understanding of the human brain is at least partly informed by their understanding of machines. The situation is not helped—either for the general public or specialists—by the rather slow development of a coherent philosophy of technology (Ihde 2004: 124; see also the remarks in Iliffe (2008)).[12]

---

[11] Aspray (1990: 239) quotes part of a very interesting letter by von Neumann written in the middle of 1947 casting light on his aims and intended audience, in which he expresses the wish that practitioners would spend more time writing about the "whole 'art' of setting up complicated computing machines, of programming and of coding." Von Neumann goes on to say that "The sooner we lay the foundation for a 'literary' method by which the properties and potentialities of the ENIAC can be made known to the general scientific public, the better."

[12] Perhaps the real origin of the possibility of artificial intelligence lies with Babbage; but throughout the twentieth century, the interpretation of Babbage's work was a wicked problem, largely because, as Bullock (2008: 36) points out, a naive "Whiggish reinterpretation" prevailed; Bullock analyses the well-known but not well-understood crucial text The Ninth Bridgewater Treatise as a description of a "simulation model" (22).

3.3 "Intelligence"/"Learning"

The term "artificial intelligence" was coined by John McCarthy in 1956 when he convened the first academic conference on the subject. In 1950, Alan Turing defined machine intelligence as possessing the capability to be indistinguishable from a human counterpart: the "imitation game" (Turing 1950: 435). In the game, the human and computer must answer a series of questions or instructions, such as write a sonnet on a particular subject or solve an equation. The test of intelligence is defined in the manner of Descartes, who "first pinpointed verbal behaviour as the crucial property for distinguishing humans from beasts, the soul-bearing from the soul-less" (Shieber 2004: 4). The flexibility of verbal behaviour is the key difference. Turing's idea of "intelligence" is broader than merely recognising logical patterns—it requires reacting to unforeseen situations that have not been pre-programmed for. One of the examples he gives is an instruction to write a sonnet (although a reasonably formulaic style of poetry), and some immediate objections raised to his test were that "a lack of idiosyncratic cultural knowledge" could "easily unmask a machine" (Shieber 2004: 8).

Machine learning is generally thought to be a subfield of artificial intelligence, and in some senses, a definition of intelligence could entail the ability to react to unforeseen situations (be dexterous in verbal form and more broadly) and improve those performances over repetition, i.e. "learn". Machine learning was defined by Tom Mitchell as a situation where "a computer program is said to learn from experience E with respect to some class of tasks T and performance measure P, if its performance at tasks in T, as measured by P, improves with experience" (Mitchell 1997). Before there were modern AI systems, there were "knowledge-based" systems, "expert systems", and "decision support" systems. All these tried to encapsulate human expertise and incorporate it into "software."

A current widely used textbook, Russell and Norvig's *Artificial intelligence: A modern approach* (2016), uses the now almost inevitable anthropomorphic language carefully and also tries to address the problem by interleaving discussion of the philosophical foundations with the technical material (it devotes a 30-page introductory chapter to a critical history of AI, and, in the penultimate chapter, there is a discussion of the philosophical foundations). On the other hand, another standard textbook on machine learning, Alpaydin's *Machine Learning* (3rd edition 2014; but now in its 4th edition at 2020), opens the author's Preface with the confident statement that what machine learning produces is *knowledge*. The Preface goes on to explain that "big data" contains "hidden models" which it is the business of the complex algorithms of machine learning to ferret out and discover the value in, and adds that "smart people" will do this.

Even *knowledge*, however, is quite different from *learning*. And *learning* itself, while notoriously hard to define, from a pedagogical or cognitive science perspective is a series of more complex processes and outcomes than anything a machine algorithm is capable of (which should better be described perhaps as "optimisation" or "generation of increasingly accurate outcomes" on a specific task such as classification).

Some artificial intelligence claims to replicate human "reasoning", and historically this, according to Derek Edwards, "proceeded largely in terms of formal logic" as a convenient stand-in for "how people think, or should think" (Edwards 1997: 3). Formal logic requires a special language free from ambiguities, much like a programming language ("if p then q"). But in the real world, the formal logic of language and reasoning is obscured by "errors, hesitations, false starts" (3) as it is *diffracted* by the processes of human cognition in all their infinite variations. Rule-based intelligence completely misses out other, equally valid aspects of intelligence, such as emotional intelligence or empathy, which are required to interpret communication.

In the article "What is Learning Anyway?" (Alexander et al. 2009), the authors define the following principles of learning:

1 Learning is change
2 Learning is inevitable, essential, and ubiquitous
3 Learning can be resisted
4 Learning may be disadvantageous
5 Learning can be tacit and incidental as well as conscious and intentional
6 Learning is framed by our humanness
7 Learning refers to both a process and a product
8 Learning is different at different points in time
9 Learning is interactional.

From this, we can gather that there is more to learning than improving one's performance on particular tasks with experience, and it is not confined to rational thinking. Learning is a more holistic activity linked to survival and involves our "neurobiological architecture" and senses that interact with the world.

Let us consider, for example, search engines. We will begin by describing how machine learning is implemented in search engine query results ranking, and then return to compare this process to the principles of human learning discussed above. While the large commercial search engine companies such as Google do not publicly release their search ranking algorithms, we can consider ranking algorithms that have been discussed in computer science literature.

In recent years, the approaches to search query result rankings generally fall into a category of machine learning called "learning to rank". The basic idea, as outlined for example in Niu et al. (2017), is that a model is trained on a data set consisting of a query, a result for that query, decomposed into a vector of features, and a relevance score, usually provided by a human. For web page results, for example, the vector of features might include things such as the number of incoming links, the results of a previously run spam-classification algorithm (e.g. percent likelihood that the page is spam), the time the page takes to load, whether the search term appears in the title, whether the page is optimised for mobile devices, etc. With such a training set, the task is reduced to a regression problem, where the model tries to set optimal weights to each factor in the results vector, such that it can predict a human's relevance classification. Some approaches instead attempt to train the model to correctly order any given pair of webpage results, using binary classification (determining the probability that the relative ordering of the pair is correct), as this still achieves an optimum ranking without the need to assign any individual webpage a numerical relevance score. Pairwise binary classification of this kind, using a neural net, is the approach used in RankNet (Burges et al. 2005; Burges 2010), which is believed to be used by Bing (Xu et al. 2015).

We can break down the binary classification task even further. A neural network would take as an input layer the features mentioned above (e.g. number of links, spam likelihood, and load time). Each feature is assigned to a separate node, the nodes initially being given random weights. For each member of the pair of webpages for which we are interested in getting a relative ranking, the set of weighted features is passed to a linear layer implementing a function to produce a score. A further layer—implementing a sigmoid function which takes these two scores as input—then calculates[13] a probability that webpage one should be ranked higher than webpage two (Burges 2010).

A loss function calculates the difference between the correct answer and the output of the neural network. If webpage one should have been ranked first (i.e. the output should have been 1), but the output of the neural network was 0, the loss should be very high. If the neural network gave an output of 1, which is correct, then the loss should be 0. Using what is called backpropagation the model calculates which parts of the network were responsible for how much of the loss and can then adjust the weights and any other parameters in the functions to decrease this loss on a subsequent iteration. After many iterations, the loss no longer decreases greatly, and the weights remain relatively stable. The model can then assign these weights to a list of features from a previously unseen pair of webpages to determine their appropriate relative ranking.

Let us now return to the defining features of learning, as listed by Alexander et al. (2009) to consider which could apply to the processes described above. Some of these are true of machines as well. Principle 1, *Learning is change*, is certainly true: the model changes the weights it assigns over time; some results may even lead to the developer redesigning the model (selecting a different number of layers, different general architecture, different loss function, faster or slower learning rate). Principle 2, *Learning is inevitable, essential and ubiquitous*, is possibly also true. Given the context of the neural network, i.e. that it was specifically created for the purpose of improving at this task, yes, it is inevitable and essential that it will do so. The improvement at this task is ubiquitous in that it happens at every iteration of the model and there is no part of the model that is not designed to "learn" in this way. Principle 7 is unquestionably true. *Learning refers to both a process and a product* in machine learning, just as it does in humans.

Principle 4, *Learning may be disadvantageous* is a difficult one to interpret. In machine learning, learning is defined as improved performance on the given task, as measured by improvement in the result of the loss function over time. Therefore, if a change in the weights or other parameters is disadvantageous, by definition it does not count as "learning". Alexander, Schallert, and Reynolds distinguish, however, between learning that is disadvantageous to the learner (which is like a change in the weights which does not produce a better output), and learning that is disadvantageous to society. It is certainly the case that a page ranking model could improve its page ranking to the satisfaction of its programmer, i.e. better matching of the training data input, yet cause overall disadvantage to society when implemented (e.g. by ranking highly pages that contain fake news, violence, or other problematic content).

---

[13] Note that Burges (2010: 2) himself says "a learned probability" for what is a calculation—a function within the capacity of someone with high school mathematics to understand (the first formula on page 2).

The remaining principles, however, are where the difference between human learning and machine "learning" become apparent. Principle 3, *Learning can be resisted*, is definitely not true of machine learning. The neural net has no agency and no choice in its participation in the processes above. Principle 5, *Learning can be tacit and incidental as well as conscious and intentional*, is also not true of machines. A machine does not learn to do a task which is not taught. Alexander, Schallert, and Reynolds's examples include students who are being taught algebra incidentally learning about social behaviour in the classroom, how to staple homework, and the vocabulary for talking about mathematics, most of which are learned through unconscious observation and mimicry. Our neural net example only receives a vector of the features considered relevant to its task and does not have a wider context to learn from, nor any incentive to do so as it is being measured only on performance on the one task. It is even difficult to call machine learning "conscious and intentional" unless we consider the consciousness and intent of the programmer.

Principle 6, *Learning is framed by our humanness*, may at first seem to be begging the question. What Alexander, Schallert, and Reynolds argue, however, is that how and what we learn are determined by the specifics of our neurobiology, and therefore also vary among individuals, who may have, for example, different visual processing, linguistic, or memory capabilities from each other. Obviously, machine learning is not determined by human neurobiology in the same way, although as we have pointed out, the concepts and architectures of machine "intelligence" owe something to our ideas about the human brain. There is also less variation in learning across different machines than there is across different people. The output of code for training a neural network to rank search results should not depend on which computer it is run on. The only differences should be the time taken to get to that result, and potentially whether the code will run at all (if, for example, the computer is too old or does not have the right hardware or software setup). The constraints of our humanness on learning are therefore very different from any constraints on machines on their "learning".

Principle 8, *Learning is different at different points in time*, is also not true of machines in the same way Alexander, Schallert, and Reynolds understand it for humans. There is no sense in which a machine has life stages with different learning abilities or processes. Nor does successful learning on one task usually affect the learning process for different tasks at a later date, rendering the latter qualitatively different, since a neural net is usually developed for one purpose only.

Finally, principle 9, *Learning is Interactional*, is only true of machine learning in the most banal sense: that humans must interact with the model to set it up and to provide it with training data, the machine then provides an output, and human programmers may then choose to modify or retrain the model if they are unhappy with this output. This is very far from Alexander, Schallert, and Reynolds's conception of human learning as interactional, where "continual change occurs not only to learners, but to the context in which learning is embedded as well. Learners are influenced by, and at the same time push back, take from, change, control, and create the environment in which learning is situated" (180).

These differences provide an excellent example of how the use of human metaphors for machine concepts leads to misunderstanding. A common trope in science fiction and fear in the popular media is that an AI released or escaping from a constrained set of stimuli will rage rampant across the digital world, learning all kinds of things it was never tasked to learn, and thus gaining the ability to take control of the world around it and bend it to its desires. As we see from Alexander et al. (2009), such behaviour is predicated on an understanding of learning that is very human in nature: where incidental things will be learned, accumulation of experience makes new kinds of learning possible, and learning causes individuals to change, control, and create their environments.

4 Looking Forward

Reframing AI for social good, though a tall order given the commercial and national interests involved, can, we have proposed, be accomplished via a feminist focus on language: considering how variations of expression shape knowledge and the organisation of societal norms. This feminist epistemology (Adam 1995), or knowing how, helps us to identify the histories and contexts that shape metaphors of AI. This approach could be deployed alongside other "AI for social good" advancements which recognise a combination of ethical, technical, and sense-making strategies are required. For instance, Floridi et al. (2020) identify seven essential factors for designing AI for social good that focus upon testing in the "outside world", adopting safe-guards, engaging with users, explainability and transparency, privacy and consent, situational fairness, plus "human-friendly semanticisation": "the ability for people to semanticise (that is, to give meaning to, and make sense of) something." (1789).

Through a tour of a handful of keywords from the discourse around the digital more generally and AI in particular, we have now demonstrated how historical evolution of terminology and present day usage of analogies and idioms can lead to misperceptions and lack of understanding of technology by the broader public. In most cases, this is a result of the natural process of humans seeing themselves reflected in the world around them: anthropomorphising the machine and conceptualising themselves as part of the mechanical world. Boundaries become blurred: between data/capta and the human decision-making and filtering processes that instantiate them; between the user and the used; and between the human mind/body and the machine.

The question then becomes, how can we intervene in this situation? Language is a natural outgrowth, not controllable by will. Individual utterances are chosen by an individual human speaker but the means to express a thought is a consensus-based language from whose rules and formations a choice must be made. Nevertheless, we suggest that there are ways to influence the particular subsets of language used or available to express even quite technical concepts.

From a governance perspective, thought could be given in future research to the possibilities for a transnational body along the lines of the W3C, which has been successful in establishing web standards, through nothing more than making "recommendations". Similarly, there might be an opportunity for an organisation to recommend terminology for use by those publicly discussing AI in education or the media, or in other public settings that influence general perceptions of what AI is and can do. While attempts to politically and socially control language or language change by means of committees have historically had little success, at the current time, most people take their linguistic cues for talking about AI from a relatively small number of individuals and organisations: the major technology companies, some high-profile scientists and educators, or journalists and fiction writers who are influenced by these technologists. This could be turned to an advantage in that recommendations for terminology would only need to be adopted by relatively few entities to have very large effects.

Language cannot entirely be left in the hands of committees and official recommendations, however. Language naturally evolves, and new terminology or terminological change proceeds at a grass-roots level, disseminating through social networks by virtue of individual interactions. At this level, too, it is important that the language used to frame AI both accurately represents the technology and does not encode or perpetuate biases. This can then only be done by ensuring that a diverse and representative population is participating in the conversation about AI, so that a culturally and socially diverse and more broadly appropriate set of analogies, metaphors, perspectives, and technical terms become available in the first place. Until these first steps are taken, we are not yet in a position to propose a wide range of alternatives to the terminology currently in use, although we have suggested that some existing terms, such as Drucker's *capta* for "data", and machine "optimisation" rather than "learning" may be appropriate.

One of a number of challenges identified in a review of AI4SG literature performed by Shi et al. (2020) focusses on keeping the "human in the loop"; this finding resonates with the need for "framing AI"—the powerful role which language and context play in human knowledge and understanding: "AI4SG is meant to work with humans, not in place of humans […] and in almost all AI4SG applications, it is an important and common research challenge in AI4SG to study how humans and AI algorithms can work together in synergy." (41).

5 Conclusions

This paper has offered a sketch towards understanding how some AI terminology has gained currency and what its affordances and effects are. We have employed, via brief studies of a set of keywords, the methods of corpus linguistics, textual exegesis, and historical interpretation within a feminist epistemology—one which does not accept that "knowledge" and the language which describes and distributes it is owned by any one group of people—in an experimental manner.

We raise a concern that some of the ethical problems now presented by AI (and highlighted by many scholars) are a product of the language used. The key problem common to all of the examples mentioned is the hyperbolic and euphemistic terminology that implies the existence of omnipotent and irreversibly embedded technologies in human society that are beyond the understanding of an average person. The realities of these technologies are hidden behind an opaque layer of misleading and euphemistic language.

A key challenge for such political processes of transparency or a fair debate, and therefore a problem for developing AI for social good, is that the general population lacks a clear understanding of how these technologies work and what their limitations are. Moreover, gendered, racialized, and other demographic assumptions and structural barriers present obstacles for many to gaining such an understanding. As a result, there is no broadly shared knowledge about the relatively simple processes that underpin both artificial intelligence and machine learning.

The good news, however, as discussed in the final section above, is that this state of affairs provides several opportunities for intervention. Diversifying the population of computing professionals and others with a deep understanding of AI technologies will open up new cultural and linguistic sources for terminology, metaphors, and idioms that can more accurately and appropriately express the concepts of AI to wider demographics. And in turn, popularising alternative terminology (whether through transnational guiding bodies, high-profile technologists and technology organisations, or national educational or media organisations), may increase the level of understanding of AI by those who do *not* work as computing professionals. Increasing this level of understanding so that ideally, the whole population can contribute meaningfully to a debate about how and when we want to incorporate AI into our daily lives will, finally, massively increase the potential of AI for Social Good.

References

Abbiss, J. (2011). Boys and machines: gendered computer identities, regulation and resistance. *Gender and Education, 23*, 601–617.

ABC News. (2019). Centrelink robodebt class action lawsuit to be brought against federal government. 17 September 2019. https://www.abc.net.au/news/2019-09-17/centrelink-robodebt-class-action-lawsuit-announced/11520338.

Adam, A. (1995). Artificial intelligence and women's knowledge: what can feminist epistemologies tell us? *Women's Studies International Forum, 18*(4), 407–415. https://doi.org/10.1016/0277-5395(95)80032-K.

Alexander, P. A., Schallert, D. L., & Reynolds, R. E. (2009). What is learning anyway? A topographical perspective considered. *Educational Psychologist, 44*(3), 176–192.

Alpaydin, E. (2014). *Introduction to machine learning* (3rd ed.). Cambridge, Massachusetts: MIT Press.

Aspray, W. (1990). *John von Neumann and the origins of modern computing.* Cambridge, Massachusetts: MIT Press.

Austin, J. L. (1962). *How to do things with words.* London: Oxford University Press.

Berendt, B. (2019). AI for the common good?! pitfalls, challenges, and ethics pen-testing. *Paladyn, Journal of Behavioral Robotics, 10*, 44–65.

Berkeley, E. (1949). *Giant brains, or machines that think.* New York: Wiley & Sons.

Berkeley, E. (1966). *A guide to mathematics for the intelligent nonmathematician.* New York: Simon & Schuster.

Binns, R. (2018). Algorithmic accountability and public reason. *Philosophy & Technology, 31*, 543–556.

Broad, E. (2019). Computer says no: being a woman in tech. *Griffith Review, 64*, 72–82.

Buch, V. H., Ahmed, I., & Maruthappu, M. (2018). Artificial intelligence in medicine: current trends and future possibilities. *British Journal of General Practice, 68*(668), 143–144.

Burges, C. J. (2010). From Ranknet to LambdaRank to LambdaMART: An overview. https://www.microsoft.com/en-us/research/wp-content/uploads/2016/02/MSR-TR-2010-82.pdf.

Burges, C., Shaked, T., Renshaw, E., Lazier, A., Deeds, M., Hamilton, N., & Hullender, G. (2005). Learning to rank using gradient descent. In *Proceedings of the 22nd international conference on machine learning* (pp. 89–96). New York, NY: Association for Computing Machinery.

Cabitza, F., Rasoini, R., & Gensini, G. F. (2017). Unintended consequences of machine learning in medicine. *JAMA, 318*(6), 517–518.

Caliskan, A., Bryson, J. J., & Narayanan, A. (2017). Semantics derived automatically from language corpora contain human-like biases. *Science, 356*(6334), 183–186.

Challen, R., Denny, J., Pitt, M., Gompels, L., Edwards, T., & Tsaneva-Atanasova, K. (2019). Artificial intelligence, bias and clinical safety. *BMJ Quality & Safety, 28*, 231–237.

Collett, C. & Dillon, S. (2019). AI and gender: four proposals for future research. Cambridge: The Leverhulme Centre for the Future of Intelligence. http://lcfi.ac.uk/media/uploads/files/AI_and_Gender_4_Proposals_for_Future_Research_yaApTTR.pdf.

Crystal, D. (2015). The lure of words. In J. Taylor (Ed.), *The Oxford handbook of the word* (pp. 23–28). Oxford: Oxford University Press.

D'Ignazio, C., & Klein, L. (2019). Data feminism. Manuscript draft, MIT Press Open. https://bookbook.pubpub.org/data-feminism.

Davies, M. (2004). British National Corpus (from Oxford University press). https://www.english-corpora.org/bnc/.

Davies, M. (2007). TIME Magazine Corpus (100 million words, 1920s–2000s). corpus.byu.edu/time.

Davies, M. (2013). Corpus of Global Web-Based English: 1.9 billion words from speakers in 20 countries (GloWbE). https://www.english-corpora.org/glowbe/.

Didier, C., Duan, W., Dupuy, J.-P., Guston, D. H., Liu, Y., López Cerezo, J. A., et al. (2015). Acknowledging AI's dark side. *Science, 349*(6252), 1064–1065.

Drucker, J. (2010). *Data as capta*. Au, St. Gallen: Druckwerk.

Drucker, J. (2011). Humanities approaches to graphical display. *Digital Humanities Quarterly, 5*(1).

Edwards, D. (1997). *Discourse and cognition*. London: Sage.

Ensmenger, N. (2004). Power to the people: toward a social history of computing. *IEEE Annals of the History of Computing, 26*(1), 94–96.

Floridi, L., Cowls, J., King, T. C., & Taddeo, M. (2020). How to design AI for social good: Seven essential factors. *Science and Engineering Ethics, 26*, 1771–1796. https://doi.org/10.1007/s11948-020-00213-5.

Goldstine, H. H. (1993). *The computer: from Pascal to von Neumann*. Princeton: Princeton University Press.

Gookin, D. (2013). *PCs for dummies*. Hoboken: John Wiley & Sons.

Haviland, W. A., Prins, H. E., & McBride, B. (2013). *Anthropology: the human challenge*. Boston: Cengage Learning.

Hicks, M. (2017). *Programmed inequality: how Britain discarded women technologists and lost its edge in computing*. Cambridge, MA: MIT Press.

Ihde, D. (2004). Has the philosophy of technology arrived? A state-of-the-art review. *Philosophy of Science, 71*(1), 117–131.

Iliffe, R. (2008). History of science. archives.history.ac.uk/makinghistory/resources/History_of_Science_fullversion.pdf.

Joos, I., Nelson, R., & Wolf, D. (2019). *Introduction to computers for healthcare professionals*. Burlington: Jones & Bartlett Publishers.

Kukutai, T., & Taylor, J. (Eds.). (2016). *Indigenous data sovereignty: toward an agenda* (Vol. 38). Canberra: ANU Press.

Leavy, S. (2018). Gender bias in artificial intelligence: the need for diversity and gender theory in machine learning. *Proceedings of the 1st International Workshop on Gender Equality in Software Engineering, ACM*, pp. 14–16.

Levinson, S. C. (1997). Language and cognition: The cognitive consequences of spatial description in Guugu Yimithirr. *Journal of Linguistic Anthropology, 7*(1), 98–131.

Leybourn, T. (1802). *A synopsis of data for the construction of triangles*. London: Glendinning.

Lie, M. (1995). Technology and masculinity: The case of the computer. *European Journal of Women's Studies, 2*(3), 379–394.

Lindqvist, A., Renström, E. A., & Sendén, M. G. (2019). Reducing a male bias in language? Establishing the efficiency of three different gender-fair language strategies. *Sex Roles, 81*(1–2), 109–117.

Madras, D., Creager, E., Pitassi, T., & Zemel, R. (2019). Fairness through causal awareness: learning causal latent-variable models for biased data. In *Proceedings of the conference on fairness, accountability, and transparency* (pp. 349–358). New York, NY: Association for Computing Machinery.

Margolis, J., & Fisher, A. (2002). *Unlocking the clubhouse: women in computing*. Cambridge, MA: MIT Press.

Mendick, H., & Moreau, M.-P. (2013). New media, old images: constructing online representations of women and men in science, engineering and technology. *Gender and Education, 25*(3), 325–339.

Mitchell, T. M. (1997). *Machine learning*. New York: McGraw Hill.

Mitchell, M., Wu, S., Zaldivar, A., Barnes, P., Vasserman, L., Hutchinson, B., Spitzer, E., Raji, I. D., & Gebru, T. (2019). Model cards for model reporting. In *Proceedings of the conference on fairness, accountability, and transparency* (pp. 220–229). New York, NY: Association for computing machinery.

Niu, H., Keivanloo, I., & Zou, Y. (2017). Learning to rank code examples for code search engines. *Empirical Software Engineering, 22*(1), 259–291.

Okolloh, O. (2009). Ushahidi, or 'testimony': Web 2.0 tools for crowdsourcing crisis information. *Participatory Learning and Action, 59*(1), 65–70.

Oldenziel, R. (1999). *Making technology masculine: men, women and modern machines in America*. Amsterdam: Amsterdam University Press.

Pechtelidis, Y., Kosma, Y., & Chronaki, A. (2015). Between a rock and a hard place: Women and computer technology. *Gender and Education, 27*(2), 1–19.

Powles, J., with Nissenbaum, H. (2018). The seductive diversion of "solving" bias in artificial intelligence. Medium. 8 December 2018. https://medium.com/s/story/the-seductive-diversion-of-solving-bias-in-artificial-intelligence-890df5e5ef53.

Quong, J. (2013). Public reason. *The Stanford Encyclopedia of Philosophy* (Summer 2013 edition), Edward N. Zalta (Ed.), https://plato.stanford.edu/archives/sum2013/entries/public-reason/.

Roos, T. (2019). Elements of AI. Online Course. Reaktor & University of Helsinki. https://www.elementsofai.com.

Roth, L. (2013). The fade-out of Shirley, a once-ultimate norm: colour balance, image technologies, and cognitive equity. In R. E. Hall (Ed.), *The melanin millennium* (pp. 273–286). Dordrecht: Springer.

Russell, S. J., & Norvig, P. (2016). *Artificial intelligence: a modern approach*. Upper Saddle River: Pearson.

Russo, S. (1957). Data vs. Capta or Sumpta. *American Psychologist, 12*(5), 283–284.

Shi, Z. R., Wang, C., & Fang, F. (2020). Artificial intelligence for social good: A survey. *Ground AI*. https://www.groundai.com/project/artificial-intelligence-for-social-good-a-survey/1.

Shieber, S. M., ed. (2004). *The Turing test: verbal behavior as the hallmark of intelligence*. Cambridge, MA: MIT Press.

Steels, L. (2007). Fifty years of AI: from symbols to embodiment—and back. In *50 years of artificial intelligence* (pp. 18–28). Berlin, Heidelberg: Springer.

Sumner, J. (2014). Defiance to compliance: visions of the computer in postwar Britain. *History and Technology, 30*(4), 309–333.

Turing, A. (1950). Computing machinery and intelligence. *Mind, 59*(236), 433–460.

Turkle, S. (2005). *The second self: computers and the human spirit*. Cambridge, MA: MIT Press.

Von Neumann, J. (1958). *The computer and the brain*. Yale University Press.

Wempen, F. (2014). *Computing fundamentals: Introduction to computers*. Hoboken: John Wiley & Sons.

West, S. M. Whittaker, M. & Crawford, K. (2019). Discriminating systems: gender, race and power in AI. White Paper. AI Now Institute. https://ainowinstitute.org/discriminatingsystems.html.

Wood, J., & Silver, D. (1995). *Joint application development*. New York: John Wiley & Sons.

Xu, J., Zhou, S., Chen, H., & Li, P. (2015). A sample partition method for learning to rank based on query-level vector extraction. In *2015 International Joint Conference on Neural Networks (IJCNN)* (pp. 1–7). IEEE.

Zarkadakis, G. (2015). *In our own image: will artificial intelligence save or destroy us?* New York: Random House.

Publisher's Note Springer Nature remains neutral with regard to jurisdictional claims in published maps and institutional affiliations.

Philosophy & Technology (2021) 34 (Suppl 1):S45–S63
https://doi.org/10.1007/s13347-020-00416-5

RESEARCH ARTICLE

Artificial Interdisciplinarity: Artificial Intelligence for Research on Complex Societal Problems

Seth D. Baum[1]

Received: 16 September 2019 / Accepted: 3 July 2020 / Published online: 16 July 2020
© Springer Nature B.V. 2020

Abstract

This paper considers the question: In what ways can artificial intelligence assist with interdisciplinary research for addressing complex societal problems and advancing the social good? Problems such as environmental protection, public health, and emerging technology governance do not fit neatly within traditional academic disciplines and therefore require an interdisciplinary approach. However, interdisciplinary research poses large cognitive challenges for human researchers that go beyond the substantial challenges of narrow disciplinary research. The challenges include epistemic divides between disciplines, the massive bodies of relevant literature, the peer review of work that integrates an eclectic mix of topics, and the transfer of interdisciplinary research insights from one problem to another. Artificial interdisciplinarity already helps with these challenges via search engines, recommendation engines, and automated content analysis. Future "strong artificial interdisciplinarity" based on human-level artificial general intelligence could excel at interdisciplinary research, but it may take a long time to develop and could pose major safety and ethical issues. Therefore, there is an important role for intermediate-term artificial interdisciplinarity systems that could make major contributions to addressing societal problems without the concerns associated with artificial general intelligence.

Keywords Artificial intelligence · Interdisciplinary research · Automated content analysis · Artificial general intelligence

1 Introduction

This paper explores the question of how artificial intelligence (AI) can be of value to interdisciplinary research (IDR) aimed at addressing major societal problems such as public health, environmental protection, and emerging technology governance. These

---

Chapter 4 was originally published as Baum, S. D. Philosophy & Technology (2021) 34 (Suppl 1):S45–S63. https://doi.org/10.1007/s13347-020-00416-5.

✉ Seth D. Baum
    seth@gcrinstitute.org

[1] Global Catastrophic Risk Institute, PO Box 40364, Washington, DC 20016, USA

Reprinted from the journal

problems are highly complex and multifaceted and do not fit neatly into traditional academic disciplines. For example, the study of global warming integrates environmental science, social science, policy, energy engineering, and more. This extreme breadth makes IDR a very difficult cognitive challenge for even the most capable human researchers. If AI can help meet this challenge, that could be of considerable value for addressing many major societal problems.

This paper is especially interested in the possibilities for near- to intermediate-term AI systems that use existing AI techniques or relatively straightforward extensions of them. These would ideally be systems that computer scientists could work toward right now, and that would also be well short of strong AI, i.e., human-level or super-human-level artificial general intelligence (AGI). A central question of this paper is: *Can we imagine tractable, real-world AI system designs that would make significant contributions to understanding and addressing complex and important societal problems, but without posing the major risks and ethical issues associated with strong AI?* I humbly acknowledge that I do not know the answer to this question, but I do know that it is a worthy question to ask, and I can lay out some relevant considerations. That is the aim of this paper.

To streamline the discussion, let us introduce the following term:

Artificial interdisciplinarity (A-ID): Artificial intelligence that performs interdisciplinary research or supports other agents in the performance of interdisciplinary research.

Some emphasis is warranted on the clause "or supports other agents in the performance of." Per this definition, an AI system that human researchers use to perform IDR counts as A-ID. Given this wider definition, it follows that there is A-ID in active use right now. Likewise, ideas for new forms of A-ID can leverage human collaboration. To make a valuable contribution to addressing societal problems, A-ID only needs to help with some aspect of IDR; it does not need to be able to complete IDR projects with no human collaboration. Indeed, it is plausible that an A-ID system that could succeed at the full range of IDR tasks would need to be strong AI.

As a scholarly contribution, this paper sits at the intersection of literatures on IDR and both near-term and long-term AI, as well as the nascent concept of intermediate-term AI. Regarding IDR, there is an active line of research on the cognitive challenges faced by human interdisciplinary researchers (Bracken and Oughton 2006; Keestra 2017; MacLeod 2018). To the best of my knowledge, this literature has not yet considered the current or potential future role of AI. Regarding near-term AI, an extensive literature applies existing AI tools to support the research process. Most of this is oriented toward narrow disciplinary research, but some studies involve IDR (Nunez-Mir et al. 2017; Tuhkala et al. 2018). There is also a more general, extensive, and longstanding use of computers in IDR, especially in the physical sciences (Crease 2017), though that is beyond the scope of this paper. Regarding long-term AI, some studies consider the prospect of superintelligent AI designed as "oracles" to answer a wide range of questions that humans might have, some of which are in the domain of IDR (Armstrong et al. 2012; Yampolskiy 2012). Each of these lines of research is discussed in greater detail later in the paper. Finally, recent research has argued that intermediate-term AI has gone overlooked relative to near-term and long-term AI (Parson et al. 2019a, 2019b; Baum 2020). This paper provides dedicated attention to intermediate-term AI and concurs that this time period merits attention.

The paper also seeks to encourage AI research to orient itself toward addressing important societal problems and to provide some direction for this. At present, much of AI research is instead oriented toward more intellectual goals of expanding the capacity of AI systems or toward profitable activities of technology corporations. As is well-known in a lot of IDR, intellectual progress and profit do not necessarily bring progress on societal problems and in some cases can make the problems worse, for example, intellectual progress on dangerous technologies and profitable activity that pollutes the environment. IDR is also not necessarily good for society and can be oriented toward a wide range of ends including intellectual progress and profit. Furthermore, even when IDR is focused on addressing societal problems, it is still not a panacea for them—the existence of literature addressing societal problems does not on its own ensure that the problems actually get addressed. That said, IDR is vital for addressing complex societal problems, and this is the primary focus of IDR today. The paper therefore encourages A-ID research to join forces with the extensive communities of IDR focused on addressing societal problems.

I approach the topic of AI and IDR as a veteran interdisciplinary researcher with some knowledge of both AI and the meta-study of IDR. I am not a computer scientist, and so I can speak with less confidence on what the AI options for IDR may be. Therefore, this paper seeks to lay out some general considerations and to hopefully serve as a prompt for an interdisciplinary conversation among computer scientists, scholars of IDR, and others with relevant perspectives. As this paper explains, this sort of interdisciplinary conversation can be difficult, but it is vital for making progress on a wide range of cross-cutting topics.

In keeping with much of the literature on IDR, this paper is written in terms of "societal problems" instead of the concept of "social good" that frames this special issue. These two terms are broadly compatible, in that addressing societal problems is one major way to advance the social good. IDR is commonly used to make progress on specific problems or issues, and is perhaps less commonly used to understand or advance the good in a more abstract or general sense. The challenge of understanding the complex and distinctive features of many specific societal problems is a primary focus of IDR.

As the first dedicated discussion of A-ID, the paper provides a broad discussion. Section 2 introduces IDR and outlines its cognitive challenges. Sections 3–5 discuss A-ID over the near-term, intermediate-term, and long-term. Section 6 discusses issues raised by A-ID. Section 7 concludes with general thoughts on the role of AI in addressing societal problems.

Sections 3–5 are organized around time scales because each time scale poses distinct issues for A-ID. Near-term AI can be defined as AI that currently exists or could exist in the near future via relatively straightforward extensions of current AI systems. Attention to near-term A-ID includes description of existing A-ID systems and prospects for extending them. Intermediate-term AI goes beyond what is already feasible or now in development, but it stops short of the more extreme forms of AI that could exist over the long term. This paper defines long-term AI as AI with capabilities that equal or exceed human cognition; terms for this include strong AI, human-level AI, artificial general intelligence, ultraintelligence, and superintelligence. Discussions of AI are often divided between the near term and the long term, with some debate over which is more important (Baum 2018; Cave and Ó hÉigeartaigh 2019; Prunkl and

Whittlestone 2020). Less attention has been paid to AI over intermediate time scales (Parson et al. 2019a, 2019b), though this paper finds that A-ID at all time scales can be important.

2 Interdisciplinary Research and its Cognitive Challenges

IDR has been defined in a variety of ways (Klein 2017). One notable definition is provided in the US National Academies report *Facilitating Interdisciplinary Research*:

Interdisciplinary research (IDR) is a mode of research by teams or individuals that integrates information, data, techniques, tools, perspectives, concepts, and/or theories from two or more disciplines or bodies of specialized knowledge to advance fundamental understanding or to solve problems whose solutions are beyond the scope of a single discipline or area of research practice (Committee on Facilitating Interdisciplinary Research and Committee on Science, Engineering, and Public Policy 2005, p.2).

Interdisciplinarity is often compared with related concepts, especially multidisciplinarity and transdisciplinarity. To generalize, multidisciplinary research is commonly understood to be the closest to disciplinary research, consisting of research that has input from multiple disciplines without integrating them; IDR takes an additional step away from disciplinary research by also integrating insights from across disciplines; transdisciplinary research is the furthest from disciplinary research by transcending disciplinary boundaries altogether, as if they did not exist, and often also transcending boundaries between academic and nonacademic sources of knowledge. These distinctions are fuzzy and contested (Klein 2017) but suffice for purposes of this paper. Note that some of the research described in this paper may be more precisely classified as transdisciplinary, though the distinction between interdisciplinarity and transdisciplinarity is not crucial for this paper and the paper will use the two terms more or less interchangeably.

IDR has traditionally had two somewhat distinct motivations. See Bernstein (2015) for an intellectual history. One motivation is intellectual, seeking the understanding of cross-cutting topics and the synthesis of knowledge accumulated in (and beyond) the disciplines. An especially ambitious form of this motivation, associated mainly with transdisciplinarity, is for unifying all of the various strands of human knowledge and intellectual activity. The concept of consilience as developed by Wilson (1998) is one work in this direction. While intellectually motivated IDR is commonplace, IDR is perhaps more commonly motivated by practical societal problems. Environmental problems have been a longstanding focus, given their societal importance and multifaceted nature, involving both social and ecological systems. More generally, IDR often—but not always–addresses social and policy issues associated with science and technology; this includes social and policy issues raised by AI.

A different type of motivation for IDR is the complexity of many important subjects of study. Complexity can be defined in a variety of ways; one definition proposed in the context of IDR is that complexity is an attribute of systems whose components—which may themselves be systems–interact in predominantly nonlinear ways (Newell 2001). I would add that while this definition's emphasis on nonlinear systems has a mathematical tone, the interconnections found in IDR are often best understood in more qualitative terms. Regardless, the definition points to the distinction between multidisciplinarity and interdisciplinarity. Many research subjects do not fit neatly within any one academic discipline, but research on these subjects does not necessarily require integration across disciplines. For example, oceanography and battery technology are both relevant to the study of global warming, but oceanographers and battery engineers typically do not need to consider each others' work when doing their own. (This example is from a critique of IDR by Jacobs 2013, p.130–131.) This disconnected work would classify as multidisciplinary but not interdisciplinarity. As a contrasting example, global warming policy may affect industrial activity, which affects greenhouse gas emissions, which affect climate patterns, which affect natural hazards, which affect human welfare. Interdisciplinary global warming policy research may consider these complex interconnections to assess the overall merits of a policy idea.

All research, whether interdisciplinary or disciplinary, has social as well as intellectual dimensions. Indeed, one argument in favor of disciplines is that they provide a useful structure for organizing populations of human researchers within universities (Jacobs 2013). Interdisciplinary research centers serve a similar social purpose. Likewise, some challenges for IDR are of a social and not intellectual nature. For example, the discipline-based department system at most universities often incentivizes disciplinary research over IDR. These social dimensions may be less relevant to an A-IDR system. AI may be more skilled at IDR than humans because AI lacks social reasons to cluster into disciplines. However, if an A-IDR system derives its knowledge from the corpus of human scholarship, then it may learn and perpetuate disciplinary divisions, just as current AI systems learn and perpetuate human biases obtained from other human-produced datasets.

The remainder of this section surveys some cognitive challenges of IDR. All forms of research can be cognitively difficult, but IDR poses some distinct challenges that make it especially challenging for human researchers. Note that these challenges also apply to transdisciplinary research and to a lesser degree to multidisciplinary research. For more general discussion of interdisciplinarity, multidisciplinarity, and transdisciplinarity, see e.g., Hoffmann et al. (2013), McGregor (2014), Bernstein (2015), Lawrence (2015), Scholz and Steiner (2015), Menken and Keestra (2016), and Frodeman (2017); for an alternative and more critical perspective, see Jacobs (2013).

2.1 Disciplinary Divides

Different academic disciplines commonly approach the same topic from different perspectives, using different conceptual paradigms and different language, featuring different intellectual traditions and standards, and often covering different aspects of the same topic. This creates the cognitive challenge of integrating the disparate input into a unified understanding of a topic (Bracken and Oughton 2006; Keestra 2017; MacLeod 2018). As a consequence, IDR requires a laborious and often frustrating process of translation between different disciplines. It is a translation of language as well as of intellectual norms and epistemic perspectives.

Much of the challenge comes from the fact that human expertise builds from years of focused study and practice. The human mind can achieve high levels of performance on specific tasks by forming complex representations of the task and its surrounding context—for example, chess masters "chunking" (Chase and Simon 1973) together complex patterns of chess pieces. The sheer difficulty of developing expertise precludes individual researchers from being expert on the full range of subjects that are relevant to complex societal problems. Furthermore, the very nature of human expertise can make it harder for experts in one discipline to understand other disciplines. Indeed, the term "discipline" implies a certain disciplining of the human mind to think in certain ways. A human mind disciplined to think in one way can struggle to think in another way.

Compounding the problem is the fact that academia is traditionally divided into thematic disciplines that do not map to societal problems. A scholar is typically trained and employed as, for example, a computer scientist or a social scientist, not as an expert on the social implications of computers. Academia has made some effort to restructure toward IDR, but the traditional disciplines still dominate. As a consequence, disciplinary divides are even greater than they in principle need to be.

2.2 Massive Literatures

Even if a researcher or research team is able to parse the disparate disciplinary contributions to a particular topic, there remains the challenge of reading the relevant literature. Even within a single discipline, literature review can be a highly laborious task. For complex interdisciplinary topics, it quickly becomes overwhelming.

For example, the Intergovernmental Panel on Climate Change (IPCC) is a body of top global warming researchers from around the world. It produces periodic syntheses of the global warming literature for high-level policy audiences. IPCC reviews are massive exercises, involving hundreds of scientists each putting in hundreds of hours over periods of up to 5 years (Victor 2015). Despite this massive scale, the literature is now at a point where the IPCC's teams of researchers are struggling to keep up (Minx et al. 2017). Climate change is an especially complex issue with a large literature even by IDR standards, but the IPCC is also an unusually large IDR project. Other IDR projects with narrower scopes and smaller teams face similar literature challenges.

The IPCC is distinctive in its effort to synthesize the entire peer-reviewed literature on a complex interdisciplinary topic. Researchers who merely wish to contribute to the literature do not need to read so much. However, gaining a basic understanding of global warming in all its facets still requires reading at least some literature across numerous subjects in natural science, social science, engineering, the humanities, policy, etc. This is an extensive undertaking, and it is compounded by the added challenge of translating across the disciplinary divides.

2.3 Peer Review

IDR poses distinct peer-review challenges. IDR commonly works at the interface of multiple traditional academic disciplines. In many cases, it is uncommon to have expertise in each of the disciplines. Indeed, the person or team performing the IDR may be the only one in the world working across that particular set of topics. For example, this paper works at the intersection of AI and IDR; I am not aware of any other research that does this.

The eclectic mixes of topics found in IDR make it unusually difficult to peer review (Laudel 2006; Pautasso and Pautasso 2010; Holbrook 2017). If no other researchers have expertise across the range of topics covered in the work, then it may be necessary to form an interdisciplinary team of reviewers, but then this team must overcome its own disciplinary divides, which is a substantial task just to complete a single review. Or, the task of working across the disciplinary divides may fall to the people handling the submissions—journal editors, grant program managers, etc.—but then this just adds to their burden.

It has been suggested that the difficulty of reviewing IDR, combined with the tendency of researchers to favor work from their own specialty, biases reviewers against IDR (Laudel 2006). One study has found that IDR grant proposals are indeed funded at a lower rate (Bromham et al. 2016). This is another way in which the current academy may be systematically biased against IDR, limiting its contribution to addressing important societal problems.

2.4 Transfer

Some research aims to transfer insights from the study of one societal issue to another. Transfer is seldom discussed in literature about IDR, which tends to focus on one issue at a time (but see Krohn 2017). Transfer is not a panacea, especially given the distinct attributes that each societal issue has, which limits the extent to which insights transfer from one issue to another. Nonetheless, it can be a powerful way to study societal issues. Transfer can be especially helpful for newly emerging issues that have not yet built up a robust literature, such as issues involving emerging technologies. For example, Altmann and Sauer (2017) transfer insights from strategic studies of nuclear weapons to the study of newly emerging autonomous weapon systems. Baum (2017a) transfers insights from the psychology of promoting environmentally beneficial behaviors among the lay public to the study of how to encourage AI researchers to pursue socially beneficial AI designs.

The psychology of transfer finds that people tend to be more successful at it when there is relatively little "distance" between the domain transferred *from* and the domain transferred *to* (Perkins and Salomon 1992). For example, it may be easier to transfer insight from one weapon system to another (as in Altmann and Sauer 2017) than it is to transfer insight from lay public environmental behavior to expert behavior on technology development (as in Baum 2017a). Unfortunately, much of the insight available to be transferred lies at a considerable conceptual distance. A major challenge is simply recognizing the cross-issue similarity. Indeed, another finding from the psychology of transfer is that people often struggle to apply lessons to "problem isomorphs," i.e., to another domain that is functionally equivalent but different in appearance (Simon and Hayes 1976). People even struggle with problem isomorphs when both domains are presented to them. IDR transfer is more difficult because researchers typically must identify the two domains for themselves. On top of that, IDR transfer can require bridging three sets of epistemic divides: the divide between the two issues and the divides within each of the two issues. This can make for an especially difficult cognitive task.

3 Near-Term A-ID

This section discusses A-ID that currently exists or could exist with relatively straightforward extensions of current technology. Note that this section takes a relatively broad view of what qualifies as AI. By narrower standards, some of what is presented here may not qualify as AI. The exact definition and scope of AI is complex and controversial and beyond the scope of this paper; for further discussion, see, e.g., Legg and Hutter (2007) on definitions and McCorduck (2004) on how the scope of what is considered to classify as AI has gotten narrower over time.

3.1 Search Engines

Perhaps the most ubiquitous form of A-ID is the search engine for Internet and scholarly databases, including Dimensions.ai, Euretos, Google Scholar, IRIS.AI, Microsoft Academic, Omnity, Semantic Scholar, SourceData, and Web of Science. Search engines are valuable for many forms of research, but they are especially valuable for IDR. In narrow disciplinary fields, researchers need to follow a relatively small body of literature. They may even be able to keep up with the relevant literature without the use of search engines, instead identifying literature by reading certain journals and sharing relevant literature within peer communities. In contrast, IDR frequently pushes researchers outside their areas of familiarity and requires them to identify relevant literature from within extremely large bodies of work.

Search engines can help with each of the IDR challenges described in Section 2. They can provide some help to the challenge of overcoming disciplinary divides by providing a tool to explore the literatures of other disciplines, though this leaves open the challenge of understanding publications in unfamiliar disciplines. They can be used to navigate the massive literatures on interdisciplinary topics, such as by searching for multiple keywords to find literature on specific themes for a societal problem—for example, "global warming" and "cost benefit analysis." They can be used to identify peer reviewers—for example, the authors of papers on global warming and cost-benefit analysis. And, with some creativity, they can support the transfer of insights across societal problem—for example, one could search for literature on global warming and cost-benefit analysis to identify insights that can be transferred to cost-benefit analysis of other global environmental issues.

Search engines could be improved. To my eyes, an important area for improvement is in the handling of synonyms and, more generally, the identification of terminology. When searching for literature on an unfamiliar topic, identifying the right keywords to search for can be a major impediment. Once one knows the right keywords, relevant literature often flows abundantly. It would be especially valuable to have tools that could identify keyword synonyms used by other disciplines. Handcrafted resources, such as Wikipedia, can be helpful, but such resources are not available for all keywords. Automated tools for this could be quite helpful.

Synonym identification is an active subject of AI research. One approach is to analyze patterns in the text surrounding a word, known as "distributional word vectors" or "word embeddings," on grounds that synonyms can be used in the same way and therefore tend to be surrounded by similar text (Leeuwenberg et al. 2016; Mohammed 2020). However, this work uses large linguistic datasets (i.e., large collections of text). Much less text is available for identifying synonyms in academic literature, especially for the many specialized concepts and small subfields. Indeed, the rarity of specialist terms can be a distinguishing characteristic of academic publications. One academic search engine, Omnity (https://www.omnity.io), uses the rarest words of a document to

3.2 Recommendation Engines

At least two forms of recommendation engines are currently available for research. The first provides recommendations of publications. For example, Google Scholar provides publication recommendations that are customized for individual user profiles, and Elsevier provides publication recommendations that are customized for specific publications on its ScienceDirect website. A more specialized example is the project http://x-risk.net that provides recommendations of publications in the field of catastrophic risk (Shackelford et al. 2020). These recommendations provide an additional way for researchers to identify relevant literature on the topics they are studying. Note that the recommendations cover topics that researchers have already identified, via their user profiles or the publications they are already looking at, so they are less valuable for the IDR challenge of exploring unfamiliar lines of research. Therefore, in terms of the challenges described in Section 2, these recommendation engines can be especially valuable for handling massive literatures, and they may be of relatively limited value for overcoming disciplinary divides.

A second form of research recommendation engine recommends potential peer reviewers to journal editors. This is used, for example, in the Elsevier Evise system, which was launched in 2015. Insofar as Evise provides good recommendations of peer reviewers, it can lighten the burden on journal editors, as noted, for example, by the editor of the interdisciplinary Elsevier journal *Ecological Economics* (Hukkinen 2017). Another example is the Toronto Paper Matching System developed for matching papers to reviewers for computer science conferences (Charlin and Zemel 2013). While the Toronto Paper Matching System is used predominantly for computer science, it potentially could be expanded to more IDR domains. The value of recommendation engines for IDR could be especially large due to the difficulty of identifying appropriate reviewers for IDR.

One way to improve interdisciplinary recommendation engines would be to streamline the process of building specialized recommendation engines. The recommendation engine presented by Shackelford et al. (2020) uses a custom artificial neural network trained with a hand-coded dataset of articles found to be relevant to the field of catastrophic risk by an open ("crowdsourced") team of researchers in the field. Other fields could apply the same approach. Hand-coding the training dataset is laborious but is vital for aligning recommendation engine results with the interests of people in the field. The labor required for this may be large, but it does not require any skills other than knowledge of the field. In contrast, developing the artificial neural network does require more specialized skills. Fields that lack people with these skills may struggle to develop their own recommendation engines. Therefore, the process of building field-specific recommendation engines could be streamlined by developing an artificial neural network that could be trained with data from any field and in particular by developing a more accessible user interface for it.

3.3 Automated Content Analysis

A final application of AI to research is the use of machine learning for analyzing the content of the literature on a given topic, known as "automated content analysis" (Nunez-Mir et al. 2017). Essentially, it treats academic literature as an instance of "big data", sometimes referred to as "big literature" (Nunez-Mir et al. 2016). Automated content analysis analyzes clusters of key words and phrases to produce statistical trends in literatures. This can be of value for learning what a literature has tended to find, where gaps may lie, etc. It can also be used for identifying relevant literature on a topic and in this capacity may be considered a form of search engine. It is of particular interest in the context of systematic reviews, in which the aim is to provide a complete and unbiased account of the literature on a particular topic. In terms of the challenges described in Section 2, this can be of high value for handling the massive literatures of IDR.

While automated content analysis has been used mainly for narrow disciplinary research, it has been used for IDR studies of forest ecology (Nunez-Mir et al. 2017) and participatory design (Tuhkala et al. 2018). The Nunez-Mir et al. (2017) study is illustrative of the possibilities. It analyzes the text of 14,855 abstracts in 7 forestry journals. It uses a mix of supervised and unsupervised seeding, meaning that central concepts are obtained via a mix of human input and algorithmic text mining. Subsequent algorithmic analysis assesses the preponderance of the concepts in the abstract database. A primary finding of the study is that most of the abstracts do not show an interdisciplinary approach and very few considered social dimensions of forest ecology. In consideration of this finding, Nunez-Mir et al. (2017) call for more IDR on forestry, especially its social dimensions.

Note that the Nunez-Mir et al. (2017) study does not reveal anything about the nature of forests or their interdisciplinary attributes beyond the list of central concepts. The output is a map of the literature, not an interpretation of what the literature means and what its societal implications are. This is a general limitation of current automated content analysis. Thus, as Sutherland and Wordley (2018, p.366) write:

Advances in artificial intelligence and machine learning could make it easier to perform tasks such as locating papers for defined topics using search terms, categorizing papers as relevant for further consideration, and producing systematic maps. But for all fields, assessing the quality of individual studies, writing up summaries and so on will continue to require skilled humans, at least for the foreseeable future.

The above remark about "the foreseeable future" suggests that the AI needed for interpreting literature and its societal implications is significantly beyond the capacity of current AI. My own judgment is that this is probably correct. Therefore, interpretation is considered in the following section on intermediate-term A-ID.

4 Intermediate-Term A-ID

Intermediate-term A-ID systems would go significantly beyond current capabilities but not so far beyond that they would constitute "strong" A-ID with human-level or superhuman-level capabilities. Intermediate-term is of interest because it could be of greater value to IDR than near-term A-ID while avoiding the downsides associated with strong

AI (see Section 5). Ideally, designs for intermediate-term A-ID would derive at least in part from existing AI techniques such that current AI researchers could work toward their development. There can also be value to envisioning intermediate-term A-ID that requires new techniques but would stop short of strong AI. Of course, the sooner new A-ID capabilities become available, the sooner they can contribute to addressing important societal problems.

As stated in the introduction, I am not a computer scientist, and so I am less confident in my thoughts on the design of intermediate-term A-ID systems. Nonetheless, a few basic thoughts on computer science factors are offered as a contribution to the topic, alongside some social factors that I can comment on more confidently.

4.1 Interpretation

One direction to extend current A-ID capabilities would be via the interpretation of research publications. As Sutherland and Wordley (2018) explain, this is a task currently left for human researchers (see Section 3.3). However, progress in the field of machine reading (a.k.a. natural-language understanding/interpretation) could change this. For example, one project to automate interpretation is the Elsevier-sponsored ScienceIE (Augenstein et al. 2017). The current focus of ScienceIE is on identifying phrases and relations between phrases within narrow disciplinary literatures. Its aims are ambitious: "Say you have a question about a paper: A machine learning model reads the paper and answers your question" (Augenstein as interviewed by Stockton 2017).

Automated interpretation of research publications would be of considerable value for many forms of research, but it may be of particularly large value for IDR, due to the large and diverse literatures involved in IDR. An integrated system for automated content analysis and interpretation would be especially valuable for synthesizing the insights contained in vast and diverse IDR literatures. Such capability could drastically reduce the burden of human researchers in IDR synthesis projects like the IPCC and could likewise enable similar synthesis projects across a wider range of societal problems. In terms of the IDR challenges described in Section 2, interpretation would be especially valuable for handling disciplinary divides and massive literatures, especially if combined with automated content analysis.

Publications can be interpreted in many different ways, some of which may be easier for A-IDR. For example, interpreting whether a publication has presented results that are statistically significant may be easier for A-IDR than interpreting whether the publication has presented results that could help address some societal problem. It may be the case that current AI paradigms based on neural networks will struggle with the interpretation of complex interdisciplinary texts because, as discussed by Marcus (2018), neural networks are skilled at finding statistical relationships in complex datasets but struggle to handle causal relationships, hierarchies, and open-ended environments, all of which are important attributes of interdisciplinary texts. However, the extent to which this is indeed the case is left as a question for future research on A-ID.

4.2 Translation

Given the difficulty of translating across the epistemic divides that exist between academic disciplines (Section 2.1), it could be of considerable value to have A-ID

Reprinted from the journal

systems that could assist with the translation. A-ID translation would convert between the jargons of different disciplines or between that of one jargon and a more widely accessible plain English. This would reduce the linguistic burden of IDR, thereby facilitating researchers to work across a wider range of disciplines, either alone or in teams. It would also be of value for peer reviewers tasked with reviewing interdisciplinary work that includes topics outside the reviewers' own areas of expertise.

Potentially, A-ID translation could build off existing work on machine translation between languages (e.g., English to Spanish). An active area of research is for unsupervised machine translation (e.g., Lample et al. 2018; summarized in plain English by Ranzato et al. 2018), in which translation does not require large datasets of pre-translated text. Unsupervised machine translation would be important for interdisciplinary translation because large datasets generally do not exist and would be expensive to produce.

A-ID translation may require techniques that go beyond cross-language machine translation because the text of different disciplines commonly varies by conceptual basis and not just by language. In other words, much of the challenge of reading text from other disciplines is that readers do not know the concepts that the words are describing or at least are not accustomed to thinking in terms of these concepts. Interdisciplinary translation is about explaining unfamiliar concepts just as much as it is about explaining unfamiliar terminology. In contrast, cross-language machine translation generally involves concepts that are familiar in both languages. For example, Ranzato et al. (2018) presents the translation of the phrase "cats are lazy" from English to Urdu; presumably Urdu speakers are already familiar with the concept of a lazy cat. Therefore, successful A-ID translation may need to include a capacity for concept identification and translation that goes substantially beyond cross-language machine translation.

4.3 Transfer

The challenge of interdisciplinary transfer (Section 2.4) maps neatly to the AI topic of transfer learning (Pan and Yang 2009). Both involve the same essential process of applying knowledge gained in one domain to another domain with similar features, especially to avoid the resource-intensive process of building complex knowledge sets for multiple domains. Complex societal problems often have some similarities with each other. Human researchers can barely scratch the surface of the potential of interdisciplinary transfer due to its cognitive difficulty and the very large number of combinations of similar societal problems. If AI transfer learning could be applied to IDR, it could open up vast possibilities for learning about societal problems.

Current AI transfer learning involves tasks that are rather far removed from IDR. For example, one common AI transfer learning task is image recognition (Zamir et al. 2018). Whereas images are readily expressed in statistical terms (e.g., via the binary representation of a digital image file), societal problems are not. To be sure, there are ways to express societal problems in some quantitative terms, such as via cost-benefit analysis for the evaluation of solutions. But much of the insight involved in interdisciplinary transfer is qualitative. A-ID transfer learning would need reliable ways to quantify this insight. It would also need some degree of translation, given the differing terminology and other linguistic constructs that can exist across societal problems.

There is some reason to believe that A-ID transfer learning could be quite difficult to achieve. Computers are very capable at churning through large numbers of combinations of predefined concepts, just as they are very capable at churning through large numbers in general. However, they may struggle at identifying the sorts of connections between concepts that humans find meaningful. In a discussion of creativity in humans and computers, Boden (2009) argues that humans are relatively skilled and computers relatively unskilled, at "combinatorial creativity," meaning creativity in making new associations between seemingly unrelated concepts. Humans have rich mental models of the world built up throughout lifetimes of experience and observation, which enable us to devise analogies and imagery and other forms of combinatorial creativity. Endowing computers with anything similar is very difficult, and computers likewise struggle at combinatorial creativity. Interdisciplinary transfer is, at least in part, a form of combinatorial creativity, and so A-ID systems may struggle with it.

5 Long-Term A-ID

As an abstract matter, it is not hard to imagine some future AI that is capable of performing the full range of cognitive tasks involved in IDR. A strong AI/human-level AGI would presumably be able to do IDR at least as well as humans could. Whereas "narrow" AI is only intelligent for a narrow range of cognitive tasks, AGI is general in the sense of being able to perform a wide range of cognitive tasks. Human-level AGI could perform the same breadth of cognitive tasks as human minds and with the same skill as human minds. Such an AI could do any other cognitive task that humans can do, so it would presumably also be capable of IDR, potentially even so capable as to effectively solve all of society's problems. The AI may not be operating in complete isolation from humans—studies of human problems would likely require some human participation—but the AI may be able to play the entire suite of cognitive roles currently played by human interdisciplinary researchers.

The prospect of solving societal problems is one common motivation for developing AGI. This is seen in the stated goals of active AGI research and development projects. For example, the AGI project AIDEUS observes that the "limitation of intellectual possibilities is fully experienced by scientists" and that this "concerns all problems of people – from traffic jams to economic crises and wars." That is very much in the spirit of the present paper. AIDEUS states this as a motivation for building strong AI.[1] As another example, DeepMind envisions AI for "helping humanity tackle some of its greatest challenges, from climate change to delivering advanced healthcare."[2] Finally, Jeff Hawkins of Numenta calls for AI to help humanity "face challenges related to disease, climate, and energy" (Hawkins 2017). Note that these and other examples can be obtained from Baum (2017b).

As valuable as AGI could be for IDR and for addressing complex societal problems, it faces several important downsides. First is the technical difficulty of building AGI. Despite the numerous projects working on AGI, the current state of the art remains quite far removed from it. It is not clear if or when AGI would be built; projections of

---

[1] http://aideus.com/community/community.html

[2] https://deepmind.com/blog/learning-through-human-feedback

decades or longer are common (Baum et al. 2011; Grace et al. 2018). That is a long time to wait for solutions to major societal problems. For some problems, such as nuclear war or extreme pandemics, the effects could be so severe that civilization would fail before it has the chance to build AGI.

The desire to use AGI for societal problems could be additionally problematic by putting a dangerous time pressure on AGI development. Herein lies a dilemma. On one hand, earlier AGI would help with other societal problems. On the other hand, a rushed AGI could skimp on built-in safety measures and ethical design, increasing the risk of adverse or even catastrophic harm caused by the AGI. To the extent that major societal problems can be addressed without AGI, this buys AGI developers more time to get it done right.

As an aside, note that some scholarship on IDR may be of value for the safe development of AGI, noting that the project of building AGI is itself an interdisciplinary task. For example, Keestra (2017) documents how a failure of interdisciplinary communication contributed to the 1986 space shuttle Challenger disaster and analyzes how future interdisciplinary communication could go better. Communication among those developing and launching AGI may benefit from this analysis.

Careful AGI design may be needed even for AGI systems that exist only to provide input on societal problems. This is a theme of the literature on the prospect of superintelligent "oracle" AIs that are designed to only answer questions that humans pose to it (Armstrong et al. 2012; Yampolskiy 2012). The oracle design is sometimes conceived as a way to make AGI safe. The hope is that by restricting the AI to only answering questions, humanity can prevent the AI from taking dangerous physical actions to alter the world. However, studies of superintelligent oracles have raised the concern that they could still be dangerous, for example, by manipulating the people who interact with it (ibid.). The prospect of strong A-ID being dangerous in this way is another reason to explore near- and intermediate-term A-ID that can help address societal problems without raising the concerns associated with strong AI.

Finally, it should be noted that the development of AGI is itself an interdisciplinary issue that would benefit from improved capacity for IDR. The development of AGI involves computer science, ethics, risk management, and more. Important questions include how best to design the AGI, how best to manage the human teams that are working on the design, and when to launch the AGI given the potential benefits and harms that could come from it. Insofar as near- and intermediate-term A-ID could improve the available answers to these sorts of questions, it could improve the outcomes from AGI development. This gives another reason to pursue near- and intermediate-term A-ID, including the concepts outlined in this paper.

6 Discussion

The limitations of near-term A-ID and the difficulties and risks of long-term A-ID suggest an important role for intermediate-term A-ID. A-ID interpretation, translation, and transfer could offer powerful capabilities for IDR and, more generally, for understanding and addressing complex societal problems. They could combine with existing A-ID systems (search engines, recommendation engines, and automated content analysis) to provide support across all of the cognitive challenges of IDR. This would not necessarily automate the full suite of IDR tasks—it could still leave important roles for human researchers—but it could nonetheless be of considerable value to IDR.

On the other hand, some of these new capabilities could push uncomfortably toward AGI. Yampolskiy (2013) argues that the understanding of natural language is "AI-complete," meaning that any AI system that is capable of understanding natural language would necessarily also be an AGI with a wide range of other capabilities. Similarly, Armstrong et al. (2012, p.305) postulate that "the task of advancing any field involving human-centred issues—such as economics, marketing, politics, language understanding, or similar—is likely to be AI-complete," and Stockton (2017) suggests that an AI capable of peer-reviewing research papers would require AGI. Exactly what, if anything, is AI-complete may be controversial and is beyond the scope of this paper, but it is nonetheless worth considering the implications of these arguments.

These arguments imply that significant portions of A-ID interpretation, translation, and transfer may be impossible without AGI. Interpretation inherently involves understanding natural language, and so there may be very little A-ID interpretation that can be done without AGI. The translation of concepts may require understanding natural language, and so, without AGI, A-ID translation may be limited to the translation of terminology. Finally, transfer may also require understanding natural language and therefore AGI unless the societal problems of IDR can be reduced to a simpler quantitative form. The extent to which A-ID interpretation, translation, and transfer can be done without AGI is an important open question.

Another concern is that intermediate-term A-ID could introduce certain biases into the research. This could occur if the A-ID interprets or evaluates research differently than human interdisciplinary researchers. For example, Hukkinen (2017) expresses concern that AI may succeed at assessing the intellectual rigor of research publications but struggle at assessing their significance for societal problems. Indeed, the ScienceIE project is explicitly framed in terms of *scientific* publications, but the interpretation of publications in other (non-science) areas that are essential to IDR for societal problems (such as ethics and public policy) require different ways of thinking and potentially different AI techniques. An A-ID system that can perform well on scientific rigor but poorly on ethics and policy could lead to weak or even harmful insight on how to address societal problems. More generally, intermediate-term A-ID systems must be carefully evaluated to ensure that they are producing constructive assistance to IDR. This will likely benefit from close collaboration between computer science developers of A-ID and human interdisciplinary researchers and potentially also people with other backgrounds, including stakeholders from outside academia.

The inclusion of non-academic stakeholders is especially important with an eye toward actually addressing societal problems instead of just advancing the academic study of them. The existence of IDR literature does not on its own imply that the problems actually get addressed. Absent close engagement from non-academic stakeholders, there is a risk of producing solutions that work well in theory but not in practice. Additionally—and importantly—engagement with nonacademic stakeholders can result in different formulations of what the problems are in the first place. For these reasons, IDR—and especially transdisciplinary research—often calls for stakeholder participation in the research process.

Readers should be aware that IDR often involves controversy, especially when it reaches out beyond the academy. Complex and important societal problems often involve heated disagreements between different stakeholders: between environmentalists and the fossil fuel industry over global warming, between rival geopolitical powers over nuclear weapons, etc. In some cases, there can be clever technical solutions that please everyone or at least do not upset anyone. However, more typically, solutions involve difficult tradeoffs between competing factions and fundamental moral values. Readers are encouraged to consider contributing to A-ID, but they should do so with an awareness of all that this entails.

In the extreme case, A-ID could even be misused so as to make societal problems worse. For example, some of the same IDR that can help environmentalists refine their messages can also do the same for the fossil fuel industry, a dynamic that may be compounded by the extensive financial resources that the industry has at its disposal. Existing interdisciplinary research communities have often handled this by engaging with the ethical dimensions of societal problems and striving for ethically sound IDR practice. Work on A-ID should do the same.

Finally, it should be noted that A-ID could help with all IDR, not just IDR on societal problems. As discussed in Section 2, IDR is perhaps most commonly performed for societal problems, but some IDR is oriented toward scientific and intellectual progress without any particular regard for societal problems. Such A-ID may be significant from the perspective of philosophy of science; this matter is left for future research.

7 Conclusion

This paper has articulated the concept of A-ID, outlined its importance for helping human researches cope with and overcome the considerable cognitive challenges of IDR, and explained how this can help address complex societal problems. A-ID exists today in the form of search engines, recommendation engines, and automated content analysis, but this leaves human researchers with the bulk of the work. Insofar as A-ID systems could contribute more to IDR, this could be a major contribution to addressing major societal problems. AI researchers interested in applying AI to societal problems may find this a worthy area of application. This paper describes some potential A-ID research directions; readers with more background in computer science than myself may have further suggestions. However, there are some difficult issues involved in A-ID that researchers should be cautious about, especially regarding the controversies inherent to complex societal issues, the potential for misuse of A-ID, and the potential relation of A-ID to strong AI/AGI. For their part, interdisciplinary researchers can contribute by using A-ID tools in their research and by contributing to efforts to improve the tools. Advancing A-ID is itself an interdisciplinary task that will benefit from contributions from people with a variety of backgrounds.

Essential IDR cognitive tasks may be AI-complete, meaning that A-ID capable of these tasks would need to be strong AI. These tasks could include the interpretation of research publications, the translation of research concepts across disciplinary divides, and the transfer of IDR insights to new societal problems. If weak/narrow A-ID is unable to handle these tasks, or other essential IDR tasks, then human interdisciplinary researchers may be largely on their own until the advent of strong AI. This would mean that, despite all the disparate ongoing accomplishments of narrow AI, it would make relatively little contribution to addressing society's most complex and important problems. Alternatively, if there could be progress on A-ID that would not require AGI, then this could be a major contribution and would be a worthy focus for the field of AI.

Acknowledgments Robert de Neufville, Roman Yampolskiy, Stuart Armstrong, Daniel Filan, Gorm Shackelford, Machiel Keestra, Mahendra Prasad, Josh Cowls, and two anonymous reviewers provided helpful comments on an earlier version of this paper. Any remaining errors are the author's alone.

References

Altmann, J., & Sauer, F. (2017). Autonomous weapon systems and strategic stability. *Survival, 59*(5), 117–142.
Armstrong, S., Sandberg, A., & Bostrom, N. (2012). Thinking inside the box: Controlling and using an oracle AI. *Minds and Machines, 22*(4), 299–324.
Augenstein, I., Das, M., Riedel, S., Vikraman, L., & McCallum, A. (2017). Semeval 2017 task 10: Scienceie-Extracting keyphrases and relations from scientific publications. Proceedings of the International Workshop on Semantic Evaluation (SemEval at ACL 2017). https://arxiv.org/abs/1704.02853.
Baum, S. D. (2017a). On the promotion of safe and socially beneficial artificial intelligence. *AI & SOCIETY, 32*(4), 543–551.
Baum, S.D. (2017b). A survey of artificial general intelligence projects for ethics, risk, and policy. Global Catastrophic Risk Institute working paper 17-1.
Baum, S. D. (2018). Reconciliation between factions focused on near-term and long-term artificial intelligence. *AI & SOCIETY, 33*(4), 565–572.
Baum, S. D. (2020). Medium-term artificial intelligence and society. *Information, 11*(6), 290. https://doi.org/10.3390/info11060290.
Baum, S. D., Goertzel, B., & Goertzel, T. G. (2011). How long until human-level AI? Results from an expert assessment. *Technological Forecasting and Social Change, 78*(1), 185–195.
Bernstein, J. H. (2015). Transdisciplinarity: a review of its origins, development, and current issues. *Journal of Research Practice, 11*(1), article R1.
Boden, M. A. (2009). Computer models of creativity. *AI Magazine, 30*(3), 23–34.
Bracken, L. J., & Oughton, E. A. (2006). 'What do you mean?' The importance of language in developing interdisciplinary research. *Transactions of the Institute of British Geographers, 31*(3), 371–382.
Bromham, L., Dinnage, R., & Hua, X. (2016). Interdisciplinary research has consistently lower funding success. *Nature, 534*, 684–687.
Cave, S., & Ó hÉigeartaigh, S. S. (2019). Bridging near- and long-term concerns about AI. *Nature Machine Learning, 1*(1), 5–6.
Charlin, L., & Zemel, R. S. (2013). The Toronto Paper Matching System: An automated paper-reviewer assignment system. International conference on machine learning (ICML) 2013, Workshop on Peer Reviewing and Publishing Models.
Chase, W. G., & Simon, H. A. (1973). Perception in chess. *Cognitive Psychology, 4*(1), 55–81.
Committee on Facilitating Interdisciplinary Research and Committee on Science, Engineering, and Public Policy. (2005). *Facilitating interdisciplinary research*. Washington, D.C.: National Academies Press.
Crease, R. P. (2017). Physical sciences. In R. Frodeman (Ed.), *The Oxford handbook of interdisciplinarity* (Second ed., pp. 71–87). Oxford: Oxford University Press.
Frodeman, R. (Ed.). (2017). *The Oxford handbook of interdisciplinarity* (Second ed.). Oxford: Oxford University Press.
Grace, K., Salvatier, J., Dafoe, A., Zhang, B., & Evans, O. (2018). When will AI exceed human performance? Evidence from AI experts. *Journal of Artificial Intelligence Research, 62*, 729–754.
Hawkins, J. (2017). What intelligent machines need to learn from the neocortex. IEEE Spectrum, **2 June**. https://spectrum.ieee.org/computing/software/what-intelligent-machines-need-to-learn-from-the-neocortex.
Hoffmann, M. H., Schmidt, J. C., & Nersessian, N. J. (2013). Philosophy of and as interdisciplinarity. *Synthese, 190*(11), 1857–1864.

Holbrook, J. B. (2017). Peer review, interdisciplinarity, and serendipity. In R. Frodeman (Ed.), *The Oxford handbook of interdisciplinarity* (Second ed., pp. 485–497). Oxford: Oxford University Press.

Hukkinen, J. I. (2017). Peer review has its shortcomings, but AI is a risky fix. *Wired*, 30 January, https://www.wired.com/2017/01/peer-review-shortcomings-ai-risky-fix.

Jacobs, J. A. (2013). *In defense of disciplines: Interdisciplinarity and specialization in the research university*. Chicago: University of Chicago Press.

Keestra, M. (2017). Metacognition and reflection by interdisciplinary experts: Insights from cognitive science and philosophy. *Issues in Interdisciplinary Studies, 35*, 121–169.

Klein, J. T. (2017). Typologies of interdisciplinarity: the boundary work of definition. In R. Frodeman (Ed.), *The Oxford handbook of interdisciplinarity* (Second ed., pp. 21–34). Oxford: Oxford University Press.

Krohn, W. (2017). Interdisciplinary cases and disciplinary knowledge: epistemic challenges of interdisciplinary research. In R. Frodeman (Ed.), *The Oxford handbook of interdisciplinarity* (Second ed., pp. 40–52). Oxford: Oxford University Press.

Lample, G., Ott, M., Conneau, A., Denoyer, L., & Ranzato, M. A. (2018). Phrase-based & neural unsupervised machine translation. https://arxiv.org/abs/1804.07755

Laudel, G. (2006). Conclave in the tower of Babel: how peers review interdisciplinary research proposals. *Research Evaluation, 15*(1), 57–68.

Lawrence, R. J. (2015). Advances in transdisciplinarity: epistemologies, methodologies and processes. *Futures, 65*(2015), 1–9.

Leeuwenberg, A., Vela, M., Dehdari, J., & van Genabith, J. (2016). A minimally supervised approach for synonym extraction with word embeddings. *Prague Bulletin of Mathematical Linguistics, 105*, 111–142.

Legg, S., & Hutter, M. (2007). Universal intelligence: a definition of machine intelligence. *Minds and Machines, 17*(4), 391–444.

MacLeod, M. (2018). What makes interdisciplinarity difficult? Some consequences of domain specificity in interdisciplinary practice. *Synthese, 195*(2), 697–720.

Marcus, G. (2018). Deep learning: A critical appraisal. https://arxiv.org/abs/1801.00631

McCorduck, P. (2004). *Machines who think: 25th* (Anniversary ed.). Natick: AK Peters.

McGregor, S. L. T. (2014). Introduction to special issue on transdisciplinarity. *World Futures, 70*(3–4), 161–163.

Menken, S., & Keestra, M. (Eds.). (2016). *An introduction to interdisciplinary research: theory and practice*. Amsterdam: Amsterdam University Press.

Minx, J. C., Callaghan, M., Lamb, W. F., Garard, J., & Edenhofer, O. (2017). Learning about climate change solutions in the IPCC and beyond. *Environmental Science & Policy, 77*, 252–259.

Mohammed, N. (2020). Extracting word synonyms from text using neural approaches. *International Arab Journal of Information Technology, 17*(1), 45–51.

Newell, W. H. (2001). A theory of interdisciplinary studies. *Issues in Integrative Studies, 19*, 1–25.

Nunez-Mir, G. C., Iannone, B. V., Pijanowski, B. C., Kong, N., & Fei, S. (2016). Automated content analysis: addressing the big literature challenge in ecology and evolution. *Methods in Ecology and Evolution, 7*(11), 1262–1272.

Nunez-Mir, G. C., Desprez, J. M., Iannone III, B. V., Clark, T. L., & Fei, S. (2017). An automated content analysis of forestry research: are socioecological challenges being addressed? *Journal of Forestry, 115*(1), 1–9.

Pan, S. J., & Yang, Q. (2009). A survey on transfer learning. *IEEE Transactions on Knowledge and Data Engineering, 22*(10), 1345–1359.

Parson, E., Re, R., Solow-Niederman, A., & Zeide, E. (2019a). Artificial intelligence in strategic context: an introduction. *AI Pulse*, 8 February, https://aipulse.org/artificial-intelligence-in-strategic-context-an-introduction.

Parson, E., Fyshe, A., Lizotte, D. (2019b). Artificial intelligence's societal impacts, governance, and ethics: Introduction to the 2019 Summer Institute on AI and Society and its rapid outputs. *AI Pulse*, 26 September, https://aipulse.org/artificial-intelligences-societal-impacts-governance-and-ethics-introduction-to-the-2019-summer-institute-on-ai-and-society-and-its-rapid-outputs.

Pautasso, M., & Pautasso, C. (2010). Peer reviewing interdisciplinary papers. *European Review, 18*(2), 227–237.

Perkel, J. (2017). Omnity opens multilingual semantic searches up to academia. *Nature Jobs*, 12 January, http://blogs.nature.com/naturejobs/2017/01/12/omnity-opens-multilingual-semantic-searches-up-to-academia.

Perkins, D. N., & Salomon, G. (1992). Transfer of learning. *International Encyclopedia of Education* (pp. 6452–6457). Oxford: Pergamon Press.

Prunkl, C., & Whittlestone, J. (2020). Beyond near- and long-term: Towards a clearer account of research priorities in AI ethics and society. In Proceedings of the Third AAAI / ACM Annual Conference on AI, Ethics, and Society, New York.

Ranzato, M., Lample, G., Ott M. (2018). Unsupervised machine translation: a novel approach to provide fast, accurate translations for more languages. Facebook Code, **31 August**, https://code.fb.com/ai-research/unsupervised-machine-translation-a-novel-approach-to-provide-fast-accurate-translations-for-more-languages.

Scholz, R. W., & Steiner, G. (2015). Transdisciplinarity at the crossroads. *Sustainability Science, 10*(4), 521–526.

Shackelford, G. E., Kemp, L., Rhodes, C., Sundaram, L., ÓhÉigeartaigh, S. S., Beard, S., Belfield, H., Weitzdörfer, J., Avin, S., Sørebø, D., Jones, E. M., Hume, J. B., Price, D., Pyle, D., Hurt, D., Stone, T., Watkins, H., Collas, L., Cade, B. C., Johnson, T. F., Freitas-Groff, Z., Denkenberger, D., Levot, M., & Sutherland, W. J. (2020). Accumulating evidence using crowdsourcing and machine learning: A living bibliography about existential risk and global catastrophic risk. *Futures, 116*, 102508. https://doi.org/10.1016/j.futures.2019.102508.

Simon, H. A., & Hayes, J. R. (1976). The understanding process: problem isomorphs. *Cognitive Psychology, 8*(2), 165–190.

Stockton, N. (2017). If AI can fix peer review in science, AI can do anything. *Wired*, 21 February. https://www.wired.com/2017/02/ai-can-solve-peer-review-ai-can-solve-anything.

Sutherland, W. J., & Wordley, C. F. (2018). A fresh approach to evidence synthesis. *Nature, 558*, 364–366.

Tuhkala, A., Kärkkäinen, T., & Nieminen, P. (2018). Semi-automatic literature mapping of participatory design studies 2006-2016. In proceedings of Participatory Design Conference (PDC'18), DOI https://doi.org/10.1145/3210604.3210621.

Victor, D. (2015). Climate change: embed the social sciences in climate policy. *Nature, 520*(7545), 27–29.

Wilson, E. O. (1998). *Consilience: The unity of knowledge.* New York: Knopf.

Yampolskiy, R. V. (2012). Leakproofing singularity: Artificial intelligence confinement problem. *Journal of Consciousness Studies, 19*(1–2), 194–214.

Yampolskiy, R. V. (2013). Turing test as a defining feature of AI-completeness. In X.-S. Yang (Ed.), *Artificial intelligence, evolutionary computing and metaheuristics* (pp. 3–17). Berlin: Springer.

Zamir, A. R., Sax, A., Shen, W., Guibas, L. J., Malik, J., & Savarese, S. (2018). Taskonomy: Disentangling task transfer learning. In Proceedings of the IEEE Conference on Computer Vision and Pattern Recognition (pp. 3712-3722).

Publisher's Note Springer Nature remains neutral with regard to jurisdictional claims in published maps and institutional affiliations.

Philosophy & Technology (2021) 34 (Suppl 1):S65–S90
https://doi.org/10.1007/s13347-020-00406-7

RESEARCH ARTICLE

Engineering Equity: How AI Can Help Reduce the Harm of Implicit Bias

Ying-Tung Lin[1] · Tzu-Wei Hung[2] · Linus Ta-Lun Huang[2,3]

Received: 2 October 2019 / Accepted: 26 May 2020 / Published online: 3 July 2020
© Springer Nature B.V. 2020

Abstract

This paper focuses on the potential of "equitech"—AI technology that improves equity. Recently, interventions have been developed to reduce the harm of implicit bias, the automatic form of stereotype or prejudice that contributes to injustice. However, these interventions—some of which are assisted by AI-related technology—have significant limitations, including unintended negative consequences and general inefficacy. To overcome these limitations, we propose a two-dimensional framework to assess current AI-assisted interventions and explore promising new ones. We begin by using the case of human resource recruitment as a focal point to show that existing approaches have exploited only a subset of the available solution space. We then demonstrate how our framework facilitates the discovery of new approaches. The first dimension of this framework helps us systematically consider the analytic information, intervention implementation, and modes of human-machine interaction made available by advancements in AI-related technology. The second dimension enables the identification and incorporation of insights from recent research on implicit bias intervention. We argue that a design strategy that combines complementary interventions can further enhance the effectiveness of interventions by targeting the various interacting cognitive systems that underlie implicit bias. We end with a discussion of how our cognitive interventions framework can have positive downstream effects for structural problems.

Keywords Implicit bias · Decision support · Augmented decision · Fairness · AI4SG · Artificial intelligence

---

Chapter 5 was originally published as Lin, Y.-T., Hung, T.-W. & Huang, L. T.-L. Philosophy & Technology (2021) 34 (Suppl 1):S65–S90. https://doi.org/10.1007/s13347-020-00406-7.

The authors contribute equally to this paper

✉ Linus Ta-Lun Huang
linushuang@ucsd.edu

Ying-Tung Lin
linyingtung@gmail.com

Tzu-Wei Hung
htw@sinica.edu.tw

Extended author information available on the last page of the article

1 Introduction

Implicit bias refers to a type of automatic stereotype or prejudice that affects our opinions, decisions, and behaviors (Brownstein 2019). Its harmful impacts include discrimination against individuals based on factors such as race, ethnicity, gender, and social class (Dunham and Leupold 2020). However, recent research reveals a growing consensus that implicit bias is subserved by multiple types of interacting cognitive mechanisms (Huebner 2016; Schwitzgebel 2013; Brownstein 2019). The complex nature of implicit bias may partly explain why existing bias-reduction interventions, which target only one or a small number of cognitive mechanisms, have limited effectiveness. This might also explain why, in turn, even the most successful interventions only seem to work in the short term (Lai et al. 2014, 2016; Lai and Banaji 2019; Liao and Huebner 2020). Given the pernicious effect of implicit bias, we urgently need to explore new intervention strategies.

One emerging intervention strategy relies on artificial intelligence (AI), the human-made computational systems capable of solving specific problems. The extensions of AI include machine learning, smart robotics, computer vision, virtual agents, etc. Chamorro-Premuzic (2019), for instance, argues that AI systems can be programmed to ignore information that is irrelevant to certain decisions (e.g., a job applicant's gender in hiring a computer programmer). This allows AI to analyze only information that is relevant to the job requirements (e.g., programming skills) in order to reach an unbiased decision. However, AI systems have been found to perpetuate bias, due to either the unintended consequences of algorithmic design or problematic data (Obermeyer et al. 2019; Richardson et al. 2019; Sweeney 2013). Pessimism about AI-assisted approaches to eliminating implicit bias prevails.

We believe this pessimism is premature and argue that "equitech"—AI technology for improving equity—has untapped potential. In this paper, we provide a framework for exploring innovative AI-assisted interventions that can effectively reduce the harm of implicit bias. "Section 2" begins with a discussion of implicit bias that emphasizes its complex cognitive nature. In "Section 3," we introduce our framework and use human resource recruitment as a case study. Using this framework, we show that existing approaches to reducing bias in hiring processes face various limitations and overlook opportunities offered by advancements in technology and cognitive research. In "Section 4," we demonstrate the utility of our framework for discovering novel approaches. Specifically, we show that our framework helps incorporate recent developments in AI-related technologies, as well as insights from philosophical and empirical research on implicit bias. In "Section 5," we show how our framework helps to design and combine interventions in a complementary way. Two implications follow from this. The first is that, given implicit bias's complex nature, it is best to combine complementary interventions to target the multiple interacting mechanisms that underlie it. Second, after endorsing the view that implicit bias involves the dynamic interplay of cognitive, social, and physical factors (Liao and Huebner 2020; Soon 2019), we suggest, in "Section 6," that interventions targeting multiple cognitive factors can have a strong positive impact on more structural problems. We conclude with cautious optimism that, despite some unresolved limitations, the future of equitech is promising.

2 Complexity of Implicit Bias

Implicit bias is an automatic form of stereotype or prejudice people unintentionally act on (Brownstein 2019).[1] It is contrasted with explicit bias, which one is aware of and/or can intend to act on accordingly.[2] Implicit bias can dispose us toward epistemically flawed beliefs and/or morally wrong decisions and actions (Holroyd and Sweetman 2016). For example, black students are often rated as less academically capable than their identically performing white peers (Hodson et al. 2002). Meanwhile, in the domain of gender, research suggests that most scientists unconsciously associate science with men (Régner et al. 2019). Implicit bias is a prevalent and pernicious phenomenon.

Notably, there is a growing sense that implicit bias has a complex nature and is underpinned by multiple types of interacting cognitive mechanisms. For example, Holroyd and Sweetman (2016) suggest that implicit biases are heterogeneous and unlikely to be captured, as has traditionally been thought, by a simple distinction between semantic and affective associations. Edouard Machery (2016) argues that implicit biases are traits—dispositions that are exhibited by various socio-cognitive skills (action, perception or decision-making, etc.) in different contexts (see Schwitzgebel (2013) for a related view). Finally, Bryce Huebner (2016) provides a cognitive architecture of implicit bias that involves multiple learning mechanisms calibrated against different aspects of our environment.

Existing implicit bias interventions tend to produce limited effects. Lai et al. (2014) examined seventeen interventions and discovered that only eight of them are effective. A recent meta-analysis study by Forscher et al. (2019) shows that the average effects of the successful interventions are relatively small. Additionally, a review by FitzGerald et al. (2019) also suggests that we need more robust data to determine the effectiveness of interventions. Moreover, most studies analyzed focused on measuring short-term changes with single-session intervention, and it is questionable whether their findings can be generalized to long-term effects. In fact, Lai et al. (2016) show that the eight interventions discussed above does not have effects beyond several hours to several days.[3] Finally,

---

[1] In this paper, we endorse the widespread view that implicit bias is a mental construct (e.g., an association, attitude, or internal structure) that causes behaviors. However, this view is not unanimously held; for instance, De Houwer (2019) proposes to take implicit bias as a behavioral phenomenon—specifically, behavior that is automatically influenced by cues that function as an indicator of the social group to which one belongs.

[2] There is some disagreement concerning how best to draw the distinction between implicit and explicit attitudes in philosophy and psychology (Brownstein 2018). In the case of implicit and explicit bias, one common way of operationalizing the distinction in scientific practice is to associate them with implicit and explicit measures, respectively. In explicit measures, subjects are asked to report their attitudes in the test, while in implicit measures, their attitudes are inferred from other behaviors (Brownstein 2019). The disagreement will not be the focus of this paper, as we believe it will not affect the arguments of this paper.

[3] See Devine et al. (2012) for a more optimistic result that shows in-person, long-term debiasing can have effects for extended periods of time. However, Forscher et al. (2017) failed to fully replicate the study.

Forscher et al. (2019) show that changes in implicit attitudes do not necessarily translate into changes in behaviors or explicit attitudes.[4]

Here, we suggest that implicit bias's complexity may partly explain the lack of effective interventions. First, current interventions tend to target only a limited number of cognitive mechanisms. Second, current interventions do not consider individual differences in the mechanisms responsible for one's implicit bias. New approaches in interventions need to be explored that can target multiple cognitive mechanisms at the same time and customize them for individuals. In this paper, we systematically examine how AI and related technology can help achieve this end. Finally, before we turn to the next section, it is worth highlighting that there is some ongoing disagreement about how best to intervene on implicit bias. While some researchers focus on its underlying cognitive mechanisms, others (i.e., structuralists) argue that what matter is not cognition but unjust social structures, which should be the main target of intervention (Haslanger 2012). Although this paper focuses primarily on "cognitive intervention," we fully appreciate the importance of structural interventions and will return to them in "Section 6."

3 How AI Has Helped: Existing AI-Assisted Approaches for Bias Reduction

In this section, we propose a framework to evaluate existing approaches for reducing implicit bias. In the next section, we illustrate the utility of our framework for exploring the solution space for promising new approaches. Specifically, we will go beyond algorithmic decisions to discuss alternative ways AI-related technology can facilitate and shape better decisions. To demonstrate how this framework is applied, we use the hiring process as a case study.

3.1 Hiring Process as a Case Study

Our rationale for using the hiring process as a case study is that it involves several phases of decision-making in which common forms of implicit bias can occur. Focusing on the hiring process allows us to consider interventions that target different types of decision-making processes as well as those that encompass the whole hiring process. Another advantage is that relevant bias-reduction technologies have already been developed and are available for investigation. Thus, the focus of our paper will be on the ways in which AI technologies, both existing and prospective, can reduce biased decision-making in the hiring process.

---

[4] Our paper focuses on AI-assisted intervention on implicit bias rather than on bias in general. Implicit and explicit biases are distinct scientific constructs, and their relation remains a topic of controversy. In addition, it is unclear whether findings in one field can be generalized to the other. For example, a recent study (Forscher et al. 2019) suggests that effective interventions on implicit bias may not always change explicit bias. Finally, implicit and explicit biases bring about different reactive attitudes. For instance, it has been shown that discrimination is considered less blameworthy when it is caused by implicit bias instead of explicit bias (Daumeyer et al. 2019). As a result, we will restrict our discussion to interventions on implicit bias to avoid complicating the discussion. However, the framework we develop in this paper can be adapted to explore intervention on explicit bias.

A hiring process is defined here as a procedure that consists of a series of decisions that are conducted by either an individual agent or a group to select new employees. An idealized hiring process typically consists of four phases. First, during the *pooling phase,* employers create candidate pools using advertisements or by actively reaching out to potential applicants. At the second phase, the *screening phase*, candidates are subject to various types of scrutiny: their resumes are screened, their skills are assessed, and other (cognitively inexpensive) strategies are used to assess their suitability. This screening process reduces a large pool of candidates to a smaller pool for the third phase, the *interview phase.* The interview phase involves face-to-face interaction, skill assessment, and other (more cognitively expensive) ways of selecting the final candidates. Finally, at the *offer phase*, positions are finalized, and successful candidates are presented with a contract, which they may choose to accept, refuse, or negotiate.

3.2 Recent Advances and Ethical Concerns about Artificial Intelligence

AI has an increasing impact on nearly every facet of our lives due to the recent advancement of deep learning and Big Data, which enables deeper integration with other technologies. One of the key capacities of AI that has widely applied is machine learning (ML). ML depends on the development of mathematical theories and algorithms that allow computers to recognize complex patterns in examples or data. For instance, artificial neural networks can be used to train a system to perform object recognition. More powerful methods can also be used to teach AI systems to make connections, hierarchical categorizations, and predictions. AI has significantly increased in power due to deep learning, which enables AI systems to recognize more complex and contextual patterns and solve previously unsolvable problems. Moreover, deep learning can be self-directed; it has the capacity, after some initial set up, to learn continuously as new data arrives without the supervision of engineers. As we will discuss below, these features are useful in real-time interactive AI applications.

Another key reason that AI has become more powerful in the past two decades is the availability of Big Data, i.e., the large amount of diverse and often continuously generated data (Sharda et al. 2020). The development of biometric-related technology has expanded the types of data that AI can draw on. A variety of sensors collect—automatically and in real time—data about such things as a person's heart rate, eye movement, etc. Some of the sensors are backed by AI-related technology. For example, computer vision can automate the processes of acquiring and analyzing visual data by producing meaningful interpretations of objects, faces, or scenes. Natural language processing (NLP), in addition, enables computers to interpret (and generate) written or spoken sentences, as well as translate them from one language/dialect to another. The challenge of processing the vast amount of data available, in turn, is addressed by the advancement of data-related theories and technologies. Data needs to be captured, cleaned, transformed, and analyzed to be useful. Innovation in data science, including the use of ML, has enabled speedy production of quality Big Data.

Ultimately, the availability of quality Big Data, together with deep learning, has led to the advancement of "cognitive computing" (Sharda et al. 2020). Cognitive computing is a type of AI system that is:

(1) Adaptive: it learns in real-time as environments and goals change.
(2) Interactive: humans can interact with it intuitively and naturally.

(3) Iterative: it can identify unsatisfactory solution and conflicting information and request or search for additional information for reprocessing.
(4) Contextual: it solves problems in context-specific ways.

These characteristics allow cognitive computing to improve the quality of the information an AI-powered knowledge-based system can provide for decision support. Moreover, it also enables AI to be further integrated with a host of burgeoning innovations, which, for this reason, we will include in our discussion. For example, augmented reality (AR) can integrate information provided by AI with the user's environment in real-time through visual or auditory equipment, such as Google glasses. Virtual reality (VR) can be combined with AI and related technologies—such as Deepfake, a technique for human image synthesis—to better create a virtual body, character, and environment. Finally, robotics working with visual recognition and NLP can produce robots that perform more complex tasks (either automatically or collaboratively with humans) and better interact with their environment as well as humans. These technologies can enhance the effectiveness of interventions by creating a more natural context in which they can occur. Some existing products for bias reduction have utilized these technologies (see "Sections 3.4, 3.5, and 3.6"). These products, however, have not exploited the full potential of integrating the aforementioned technologies with ML and Big Data (as we will demonstrate in "Section 4").

While our focus in this paper is on discovering novel and effective AI-assisted interventions, it is nevertheless important to address AI-assisted interventions' potential ethical implications. Here, we briefly review some of the pressing ethical concerns that have been discussed in the literature of algorithmic decision.

First of all, *algorithmic bias* and *Big Data bias* are two major challenges (Hajian et al. 2016; Garcia 2016; Suresh and Guttag 2019; Richardson et al. 2019). Algorithmic bias happens when an algorithm produces unfair results (e.g., the disadvantaging of people of color), even if its developers intentionally consider only non-demographic factors in coding (e.g., criminal history). This algorithmic bias happens when non-demographic factors correlate with demographic factors. Big Data bias happens when ML, without the developer's intentions, extracts patterns of prejudice that exist in the collected data. This may result in the relevant prejudice being amplified by the AI system that employs the result of ML. This happens because the Big Data can mirror prejudice existing in human society (e.g., these two challenges confront many existing and promising interventions to be discussed below and are hard to overcome completely). However, they can be ameliorated by adopting ethical guidelines for algorithmic designs and ML,[5] as well as the implementation of fairness-aware data mining and bias correction technology (Hajian et al. 2016; Lu and Li 2012; Obermeyer et al. 2019).

Opacity and *privacy* are also two critical issues that will challenge AI-assisted intervention (Taddeo 2019; Taddeo and Floridi 2018). Opacity refers to the difficulty of clarifying the causal mechanism underlying some algorithmic decisions, and this epistemological difficulty may lead to further complications regarding responsibility and accountability (Castelvecchi 2016; Floridi 2015; Samek et al. 2017; Wachter et al.

---

[5] For example, Hung and Yen (2020) extract five general principles for protecting basic human rights, including data integrity for reducing bias and inaccuracy through the examination of over 115 principles recently proposed by academies, governments, and NGOs.

2017), which will be discussed in "Section 4.3." Privacy issues happen when poor data security leads to the abuse of data and breaches in privacy, which may result in, say, threats to freedom of expression (Amnesty International UK 2018; Human Rights Watch 2019). As many of the AI-assisted interventions involve ML from personal data, it is unavoidable that they will confront these issues. However, the opacity issue can be ameliorated by developing algorithms for causal explanation or by adopting AI applications that are interpretable—as one of us has argued elsewhere (Hung and Yen 2020; Hung 2020). The privacy issue can also be alleviated by applying the well-developed principles in bioethics (e.g., those about data collection, storage, and reuse) and AI-specific guidelines (e.g., EU, IEEE, and Amnesty International) (IEEE Global Initiative 2016). For example, almost all of these guidelines highlight the principle of data security to ensure that data is under proper protection over its entire life-cycle—which helps reduce privacy breaches. We will point out the relevant ethical issues as we discuss the various types of interventions in the rest of the paper.

3.3 Two Dimensions of the Conceptual Framework

The first dimension (D1) of our framework captures the different types of information AI provides users. In decision-making, it is useful to have information about the current state of affairs (descriptive information), the likelihood of future states (predictive information), and the expected utility of an action (prescriptive information). In keeping with the practice-oriented nature of this paper, we adopt the terms commonly used in knowledge-based systems (KBSs)[6] (Sharda et al. 2020) to label our categories (rows of Table 1).

1) Descriptive analytics: KBSs can consolidate all relevant data in a form that enables appropriate analysis, characterizes data (with descriptive statistics and/or pattern recognition), and visualizes data to inform users of the current state of affairs—as well as informing users of the relevant past and current trends.
2) Predictive analytics: KBSs can provide predictions and inferences about what is likely to happen by analyzing correlative or causal relations among variables and by categorizing cases.
3) Prescriptive analytics: KBSs can provide (recommended) decisions based on what is likely to lead to better outcomes—given the relevant goals (e.g., calculating the expected utility through simulation or optimization models).
4) AI-enhancement without analytics: KBSs can assist interventions without proving analytic information, e.g., by automating the intervention, enhancing other technology involved in the intervention (e.g., robotics), etc.

Some important qualifications are in order. First, the different types of analytics are not completely conceptually independent: predictive analytics depends on descriptive analytics, and prescriptive analytics depends on predictive analytics. Second, there is a sense according to which all interventions are prescriptive, as the KBSs will need to

---

[6] KBSs are computer programs that generate information to help humans solve problems or generate solutions. AI has played an important role in enhancing the capacity of KBSs by powering knowledge acquisition, representation, and reasoning. In this paper, the use of this term is adopted from the discipline of analytics (Sharda et al. 2020). It is different from the knowledge-based system in AI which represents knowledge and performs inferences explicitly.

Table 1 Framework and existing AI approaches for reducing bias

D 2 / D 1	Input-based	Output-based	Cognition-based
Descriptive analytics	➤ Descriptive analysis of applicants' demographic information (Eightfold, Entelo, IBM Watson Recruitment)	➤ Real-time descriptive analysis of demographic diversity of candidate pool for detecting potentially biased selection decisions at any hiring phases (Eightfold, Entelo)	N/A
Predictive analytics	N/A	➤ Predicting the effect of recruiter's behavioral expression, e.g., job advertisement's appeal to potential candidates of different demographic backgrounds (Textio Hire)	➤ Predicting and inferring the qualities that make a candidate suitable rather than depending on intuitions rooted in the company's culture and practice, which may be biased (IBM Watson Recruitment, Pymetrics)
Prescriptive analytics	N/A	➤ Automated hiring decision: suggesting unbiased evaluative decisions (HireVue, Pymetrics) ➤ Automated hiring decision: suggesting unbiased behavioral expression (Textio Hire)	N/A
AI-enhancement without analytics	➤ Masking applicants' demographic information, without differentiating whether they induce bias or not (Unbias.io n.d.), Entelo, Blendoor, Eightfold) 1. Removing perceptual cues of implicit bias (Interviewing.io) 2. Creating a virtual space in which candidates can project any avatar they choose (Zaleski 2016) 3. A robotic proxy which allows candidates to control a robot to interact with interviewers (Fair proxy communication) ➤ Automatically collecting data of job applicants to reduce implicit bias (Pymetrics, Interviewing.io)	➤ Masking recruiters' behavioral expressions, without differentiating biased or unbiased ones 1. Human-free interview (Mya, HireVue), including replacing recruiters with a social robot implemented with standardized questions (Tengai) 2. Creating a virtual space in which recruiters project any avatar they choose (Zaleski 2016)	➤ Changing the associations underlying the implicit bias (change-based intervention) 1. Perspective-taking training in VR (Equal reality, Vantage point) 2. Embodying in an avatar with features of the underrepresented in VR (Equal reality) 3. Implement branching narratives in VR to practice making better decisions (Vantage point)

The first dimension (D1) represents different types of analytics playing distinctively crucial roles in the intervention. The second dimension (D2) represents the locus of intervention. In each slot, *arrowheads* indicate types, and *numbers* indicate tokens of interventions

"make a decision" to intervene (perhaps based on some implicit calculation of the expected utility of intervening, which will implicate predictive and prescriptive information as well). However, our category focuses on the type of analytics playing a distinctly crucial role in the intervention itself—because doing so helps conceptualize different existing and promising interventions. Third, our category is characterized at a high-level of abstraction in order to encompass different and more specific ways of producing analytic information. We leave the specifics open because KBSs can in principle incorporate various different techniques of producing analytics, each of which is appropriate under different contexts.

The second dimension (D2) focuses on the locus of intervention. AI technology can intervene at the different loci of decision-making: at the input, output, and cognition stages of a decision-making process. As a result, interventions are categorized accordingly (columns of Table 1):

(1) *Input-based interventions* reduce implicit bias by managing input information for decision-making. Input information includes perceptual information about an interviewee or the content of an applicant's resume.

(2) *Output-based interventions* manage the output of a biased decision-making process in order to reduce or prevent its harmful effects. Here, examples of output are discriminatory phrases in job ads, unfair evaluative judgments of a resume, sexist speech, and microaggressive behavior[7] toward an applicant, etc.

(3) *Cognition-based interventions* directly target the cognitive processes underlying implicit bias, e.g., training programs that reduce users' biased automatic associations (e.g., of "white" with "good").

By categorizing interventions into these three types, we do not imply that one can think of the input, output, and cognition related to implicit bias independently—rather, they are part of an interactive process. However, by identifying them as distinct loci of intervention in a process, we can better conceive of different possibilities for intervening on bias.

Having introduced the two dimensions of our framework, we will use this framework to assess existing approaches in the following three sections. Currently there are a variety of commercial products as well as proposals for AI-assisted intervention. We systematically evaluate them by categorizing them into types and by placing them within the solution space our framework maps out. Our framework classifies approaches into twelve types (Table 1). Our review will show that eight types of interventions currently exist but require further development. In addition, four types are unexplored and hold potential in the future.

3.4 Existing Input-Based Interventions

We will first review input-based interventions (Table 1, 2nd column). The current approaches take advantage of *descriptive* analytics as well as AI enhancement without analytics. Descriptive, input-based interventions use data visualization and analyze applicants' data to categorize and create labels for candidates' characteristics. The categories or labels include demographic information such as gender, ethnicity, and veteran status (e.g., Eightfold ("Talent Diversity," n.d.), IBM Watson Recruitment (n.d.), Entelo ("Entelo Platform Reports," n.d.)). These interventions provide descriptive information that facilitates the recruiters' understanding of the candidate pool—as

---

[7] Microaggressions are "brief and commonplace daily verbal, behavioral, or environmental indignities, whether intentional or unintentional, that communicate hostile, derogatory, or negative racial slights and insults toward people of [underrepresented groups]" (Sue et al. 2007, p. 271). Examples include talking over interviewees with a particular demographic background and insensitive comments demeaning interviewee's heritage or identity.

well as facilitating the search for diverse candidates—and can be used to track underrepresented candidates in the hiring process.

There are two types of existing interventions that benefit from AI's enhancement without relying on analytic information. The first, sometimes referred to as *anonymization*, involves masking demographic information about an applicant that can potentially induce implicit biases. It can be implemented at the screening phase, by automating the process of covering up demographic information in resumes. It can also be implemented at the interview phase by employing a robotic proxy that allows candidates to use a robot to interact with interviewers (e.g., Fair proxy communication (Seibt and Vestergaard 2018; Skewes et al. 2019)), or by creating a virtual space in which recruiters and candidates can project an avatar of their own choosing.[8]

The second type of intervention, in contrast, involves automatically collecting data about applicants so that it is less likely to implicate human bias in the data collected. This type of intervention includes automating the evaluation of the candidate's performances and capacities through the KBSs. Candidates may be asked to participate in activities that assess their professional skills (e.g., automated, coding-challenge-based interview provided by Interviewing.io (n.d.)) or their psychological traits (e.g., Pymetrics (n.d.) uses neuroscience-based games to assess candidates' memory capacity, learning skills, speed of reaction, etc.).

However, the above interventions have limitations. Studies show that anonymous recruitment is not always effective in eliminating bias and can create additional disadvantages for underprivileged applicants (Behaghel et al. 2015; Hiscox et al. 2017): removing demographic information prevents recruiters from contextualizing important information embedded in applications. This may result in negative readings of ambiguous signals, e.g., misinterpreting a female candidate's periods of family leave or part-time work as underemployment (Foley and Williamson 2018). Anonymous recruitment may also lead employers to be more influenced by the prejudices induced by other unmasked cues. For example, research suggests that removing criminal histories without masking racial information can increase racial discrimination due to the problematic assumption of racial differences in felony conviction rates (Agan and Starr 2017). Likewise, masking bias-inducing features and responses might take away useful information for interpersonal interaction (e.g., vocal variety and vitality, eye contact, etc.). An applicant's interpersonal skills, for example, can be better assessed via such interaction.[9] Finally, due to the pervasive automation involved in these interventions, ethical issues emerge concerning autonomy, accountability, and responsibility. We will discuss these issues in more detail in "Section 4.3."

---

[8] Currently, fair proxy communication and interview in virtual space are not products; they are only proposed ideas (Seibt and Vestergaard 2018; Skewes et al. 2019)

[9] Determining which information should be masked to reduce implicit bias is difficult, and the determination needs to be made on a case-by-case basis. In the information technology (IT) industry, for example, the assessment of purely professional skills may be distinguished from other traits related to interpersonal skills (e.g., personality and coordination skills) that may not be essential to the job. So, when evaluating an applicant's coding skills, demographic cues are irrelevant and should be masked. Conversely, in other industries (e.g., insurance sales), masking demographic information could be a loss when assessing the applicant's communication styles that may be essential to the job performance.

3.5 Existing Output-Based Interventions

Output-based approaches utilize descriptive, predictive, and prescriptive analytics, as well as AI-enhancement without analytics (Table 1, 3rd column). The descriptive, output-based interventions currently available detect potentially biased *evaluative decisions* by measuring the demographic diversity of candidate pools in real time. This allows recruiters to identify when candidates from underrepresented groups leave the hiring process and provides room for corrective actions (e.g., Eightfold ("Talent Diversity," n.d.)).

Current predictive output-based interventions provide information about the likely outcome of an expressive behavior. The current approach is to predict the demographic distribution of potential candidates that a job advertisement is likely to attract. For example, the Bias Meter of Textio Hire (Textio n.d.) is a gender tone spectrum that indicates the overall gender bias of job postings. These predictions help a company adjust its job postings to improve hiring diversity at the pooling phase.

The prescriptive, output-based intervention replaces or improves human decision-making with automated decisions from KBSs. First, these systems can evaluate candidates automatically based on data collected from multiple sources in order to produce (recommended) hiring decisions. They do this without the involvement of human recruiters, which reduces the overall influence of recruiter bias on the hiring decisions. For example, some products automatically assess candidates' eligibility and recommend a short-list based on their performance (e.g., Pymetrics (n.d.), HireVue ("CodeVue Offers Powerful New Anti-Cheating Capability in Coding Assessment Tests," 2019)). Also, some systems can produce or suggest unbiased behavioral expressions. For example, Textio Hire can suggest neutral synonyms to replace biased phrases (Textio n.d.).

Finally, there are AI-enhanced (without analytics), output-based interventions that mask recruiter's behavioral expression without differentiating biased from unbiased expressions. The biased behavioral output of recruiters, including biased phrases and microaggressive behaviors (e.g., reduced eye contact with interviewers), can lead to unfair results which are difficult to detect. One example of this is the self-fulfilling influence of social stereotypes on dyadic social interaction (Biggs 2013; Snyder et al. 1977): interviewers can have different styles of interaction based on their stereotypes toward candidates. Their different interaction styles can, in turn, elicit different behaviors from candidates consistent with the interviewers' initial stereotypes, e.g., interviewers' cold and distant treatment toward candidates whom they find less favorable can discourage the candidates from acting in a sociable manner. Automated interviews can mask some of the recruiters' behavioral expressions so as to reduce unfair results (e.g., Mya ("Meet Mya," n.d.), HireVue ("HireVue Video Interviewing Software," n.d.)). Similarly, the technology for masking the bias-inducing cues of applicants can be used to mask recruiters' behavioral expressions as well (e.g., using VR to create avatars for interview (Zaleski 2016)).

However, output-based interventions face limitations too. First, no existing product offers real-time masking of recruiters' microaggressive behaviors at the *interview phase*. Furthermore, even if such intervention is created, it will likely face problems similar to input-based interventions that mask applicant's information: masking (without distinguishing biased or unbiased behavior) may remove too much information from interpersonal interactions (e.g., eye contact, facial expression) for reliable assessment of communicative skills. Second, human-free interviews have similar limitations. The robot interviewer may not be natural enough because it is automated with fixed scripts and will not be able to assess interpersonal skills.[10] Finally, output based interventions that rely on automated decision face potential challenges such as algorithmic bias, Big Data bias, and the issue of opacity (see "Section 3.2").

3.6 Existing Cognition-Based Interventions

Cognition-based intervention aims to directly affect agents' cognitive processing (Table 1, 4th column). First, predictive, cognition-based interventions infer the qualities that make a candidate eligible through analyzing the characteristics of the top performers of a given position (e.g., IBM Watson Recruitment Success Score (n.d.), Pymetrics (n.d.)). As such, the qualities for successful candidates are not determined by bias-prone intuitions that are rooted in the company's culture and practice.

Second, existing AI-enhanced (without analytics), cognition-based interventions are change-based. The goal of change-based interventions is to alter the associations underlying implicit biases (Brownstein 2019). For example, taking the perspective of a member of a stereotyped group has been shown to reduce relevant implicit bias (Galinsky and Moskowitz 2000). Some existing interventions utilize VR to create training programs that allow users to adopt the perspective of the underrepresented by embodying an avatar with the relevant features to facilitate bias-reduction (e.g., Equal Reality (n.d.), Vantage point (n.d.)). The other intervention engages users in VR-enhanced real-world scenarios where implicit bias might occur to help users practice making better decisions (e.g., Vantage point (Holpuch and Solon 2018)).

There are some limitations to the effectiveness of these change-based interventions. While Peck et al. (2013) have found that dark-skinned embodiment intervention reduces implicit bias, it is empirically unclear whether this method can be generalized to address other biased factors. In addition, there are worries that the effect of change-based intervention is only small or short term and that changes in implicit associations will not translate into changes in explicit bias or behaviors that maintain intergroup disparities outside of the laboratory setting (Forscher et al. 2019).

In sum, recent advances in AI and related technology have provided us with opportunities for creating a more equitable society. We have examined existing approaches and discussed their limitations. Next, we demonstrate how our framework can help explore new approaches that can overcome some of these limitations.

4 Putting the Framework to Work: New Approaches for Reducing the Harms of Implicit Bias

We begin by illustrating that, by considering D1 (i.e., descriptive, predictive, and prescriptive analytics), we can discover better applications for recent advancements in AI and related technologies, in addition to discovering ways of enhancing human-

---

[10] Nonetheless, if the robot is too natural, it may trigger the uncanny valley effect—humanoid robots may elicit unintended cold, eerie feelings in human viewers (Mori 1970; MacDorman and Chattopadhyay 2016).

machine and human-human interactions in decision-making. We then show that D2 (input-, output-, and cognitive-based interventions) can help incorporate insights from recent research on implicit bias, cognitive control, and decision augmentation for devising new interventions (see Table 2).

4.1 Utilities of D1: Taking Full Advantage of the Advances in AI and Related Technology

There are at least three general benefits to exploring new approaches using D1.

Exploit the Underutilized Analytics First, distinguishing among existing interventions based on the types of critically-involved analytics allows us to see that existing interventions have underutilized predictive and prescriptive analytics (see Table 1). Our framework suggests that exploiting their full potential will produce better interventions.

Recent developments in deep learning and Big Data have enabled more accurate, quantitative, context-sensitive, and personalized predictions to be produced with a faster speed. The KBSs can generate, in real time, personalized predictions concerning (1) what types of input information causes or correlates with, (2) what sorts of biased evaluative decisions or expressive behaviors will occur, and (3) what types of cognitive processes are implicated in the decision-making (see the 3rd row of Table 2).

AI can generate these predictions with data collected from hiring processes in general (Clabaugh and Matarić 2018), as well as from individualized data acquired in an experimental setting.[11] For instance, it is possible to generate control groups and experimental groups of applicants' resumes and avatars. The two groups would be identical in their relevant qualifications and behaviors but different in their demographic backgrounds. Having set up the groups, data can be collected concerning individual recruiters' biased responses toward applicants, as well as biometric data taken when they review and interact with them. Such data could include information about recruiters' eye-movement to assess the attention they pay to information that could trigger a biased response. This data can also include information about recruiters' body language/facial expressions and spoken/written language in order to gauge any emotional responses that correlate with biased responses. Finally, we can collect information about skin conductance and other physiological data to estimate recruiters' fatigue and stress levels—which often lead to more biased decisions (Clabaugh and Matarić 2018). With this data in hand, ML (assisted by experts) can model the bias patterns of individual recruiters. This knowledge—along with the data collected during, say, actual interviews—can then be used to predict the level of bias in their evaluative decisions, as well as their biased behavioral expressions.

This type of predictive analytics can be extremely useful. Humans are notoriously bad at detecting their own biases (Lai and Banaji 2019). By outsourcing this task to AI—which can alert us when we are likely to be biased—we can refrain from making decisions, or actively

---

[11] Another example of how AI can help predict human biases is by using ML to detect biases expressed in ordinary language. Caliskan et al. (2017) developed Word-Embedding Association Test (WEAT)—a method of measuring the associations between words. Their model, trained on a corpus of text from the internet, succeeded in replicating the known biases revealed by the Implicit Association Test (e.g., male or female names are associated with career or family respectively). As a result, WEAT can potentially be developed to identify an individual's implicit bias through analyzing the text she produces.

Table 2 Framework showing potential future interventions

D 2 / D 1	Input-based	Output-based	Cognition-based
Descriptive analytics	N/A	N/A	N/A
Predictive analytics	➤ Predicting the kind of input that would cause biased evaluative decisions and expressive behaviors (See "Section 4.1")	➤ Predicting and quantifying the upcoming biased evaluative decisions and behavioral expressions in various phases (See "Section 4.1") ➤ Human-machine or human-human collective intelligence (see "Section 4.1")	➤ Predicting how a recruiter's level of bias in cognitive processing will be affected by different conditions, e.g. stress, fatigue, etc. (See "Section 4.1"). ➤ Potential improvement common to all cognition-based interventions (see "Section 4.2") 1. Adopting an evidence-based approach 2. Customizing/personalizing with better predictive (and prescriptive) analytics 3. Allowing frequent intervention ➤ Changing the associations underlying the implicit bias (change-based intervention) 1. Influencing users' multiple cognitive mechanisms through VR enhancement ➤ Helping individuals gain better control of the influence of implicit bias on their decision-making and behaviors (control-based intervention) 1. Integrating with AI-related technologies (e.g., AR) to reduce user's cognitive cost, facilitate speedy control, and combine multiple interventions ➤ Enhancing human decision-making capacities via human-machine interactions (augmentation-based intervention) 1. Focusing on natural and complementary human-machine interactions 2. Providing (descriptive, predictive, and prescriptive) information on a need basis
Prescriptive analytics	➤ Selectively masking or translating away bias-inducing information about applicants (See "Section 4.1").	➤ Selectively masking or translating away demographic information or the biased expressive behaviors of recruiters (See "Section 4.1") ➤ Human-machine or human-human collective intelligence (see "Section 4.1")	➤ Change-based intervention (see above) ➤ Control-based intervention (see above) ➤ Augmentation-based intervention (see above)

The first dimension (D1) represents different types of analytics playing distinctively crucial roles in the intervention. The second dimension (D2) represents the locus of intervention

seek out interventions, to reduce bias. Moreover, better predictive analytics can be used to produce better prescriptive analytics and relevant interventions (which we discuss next).

That said, better predictive and prescriptive analytics can come with some cost, including issues of privacy and opacity ("Section 3.2"). More accurate prediction requires more personal data; yet, the collection of personal data comes with the risk of privacy breaches. It is currently an unresolved normative question as to the extent to which a company can legally and ethically collect, store, and use the personal data of candidates and recruiters. Additionally, the manner by which ML generates results is often opaque and inexplicable (Castelvecchi 2016; Wachter et al. 2017). It is unclear whether recruiters should rely on information produced by a "blackbox" algorithm they do not fully understand.

Innovate AI-Related Technologies The second benefit of exploring new approaches using D1 is that it helps consider opportunities that new technologies (e.g., AR, VR, robotics) provide. These technologies, with the help of AI, can enhance the effectiveness of interventions by creating a more natural context under which interventions can occur. Additionally, using data captured by the various sensors, AI can deliver the intervention to the user in a personalized and context-sensitive way. For example, such implementations allow us to selectively "translate" any biased or bias-inducing verbal and visual features/ expressions of both applicants and recruiters into neutral features/expressions. This is achieved by combining VR, Deepfake, and NLP with enhanced KBSs that are capable of generating real-time predictions of individual recruiters' biased decisions and expressions (as discussed above) and selectively removing them. This intervention can produce an avatar of an applicant or recruiter in a virtual space that expresses verbal and bodily language with almost identical semantic and emotional content but which includes much less bias-inducing information of applicants or biased expressions of recruiters.

As an input-based intervention, such an approach allows us to selectively "translate away" only the information of applicants predicted to significantly trigger biased evaluation in a particular recruiter while at the same time retaining information that does not trigger such biased evaluations. One advantage is that the input-based intervention will enable the recruiter to take advantage of the remaining demographic information to properly contextualize applicants' performance and reach fairer evaluative decisions. Moreover, the intervention will allow the recruiter to better interact with applicants and facilitate proper evaluations of their relevant interpersonal skills. Both features ameliorate the limitations of existing input-based interventions that mask all the demographic information of applicants.

As an output-based intervention, this approach can selectively "translate" only a recruiter's significantly problematic expressive behaviors, again striking a balance between bias-reduction and the allowance of social interactions in order to assess relevant skill sets. As a result, this approach can overcome a key limitation of existing output-based interventions that automatize interviews or mask all of the recruiters' behavior non-selectively.

However, this new technology may invite attendant harm. Translating away interviewers' biased expressions means that interviewees lose the opportunity to recognize that their interviewers are biased and to choose whether to address the relevant issue on the spot—for example, addressing mansplaining by asserting one's epistemic authority.

This limitation may thus result in worse outcomes for the interviewee overall.[12] Moreover, by taking away important information for decision-making, it also invites ethical concerns such as AI paternalism (i.e., AI increases a human's own good at the cost of restricting their autonomy). We will discuss this issue in "Section 4.3."

Enhance Human-Machine Interactions Finally, D1 can help us explore four enhanced modes of human-machine interactions. These interactions are enhanced to the extent that AI systems, with enhanced predictive and prescriptive analytics, improve their capacity to:

1) Collaborate with humans in discovering solutions to complex problems. Recent AI's continuous and fast learning from Big Data has enabled it to interact with humans in real time, provide context-appropriate support, and complement humans' strengths and weaknesses.
2) Assist interpersonal interactions in decision-making, such as improving the quality of interpersonal communications and collective decision-making.
3) Train us to make better decisions by shaping our cognitive process in a personalized, naturalistic, and effective training environment.
4) Automatically make context-appropriate decisions for complex problems.

Consider, for example, new interventions that employ human-machine group collaborations. They are made possible based on predictive analytics that quantify individual recruiters' reliability (e.g., the degree to which they exhibit bias) in their evaluation. Aggregating evaluative decisions, under the right conditions, can lead to more reliable collective decisions than those made by individuals—this phenomenon is called the Wisdom of the Crowd Effect (Surowiecki 2005). One good way of aggregating individual decisions is to do so after weighing them by their reliability (as predictive analytics provided by KBSs), which further enhances the reliability of collective decision-making. Moreover, AI-agents using a variety of algorithms to make automated hiring decisions (prescriptive analytics) can be included as recruiters as well. This can result in a further improvement in reliability when a group of decision-makers have different backgrounds—such that their judgments reflect independently generated and divergent points of view. This new mode of intervention allows recruiters to reach less biased decisions by complementing one another's strengths and weaknesses.

However, integrating automated decision into a collective decision-making framework not only raises ethical issues of algorithmic bias, Big Data bias, and the issue of opacity ("Section 3.2"), but it also raises new issues about individual and *collective* responsibility. We shall discuss these emerging issues in "Section 4.3."

4.2 Utilities of D2: Incorporating Insights from Recent Empirical Research

As we have shown in "Section 3," D2 illuminates the fact that cognition-based interventions have been under-explored by existing approaches. However, there is a

---

[12] A possible solution to this attendant harm focuses on reducing the implicit bias of interviewers. Since AI detects bias, it can also be programmed to alert the interviewers for correction while masking the biased expressions to the interviewees. The detection record can be used by senior managers to choose better interviewers.

rich cognitive scientific literature that we can draw on to design more effective AI-assisted, cognition-based interventions. There are at least two further types of cognition-based interventions available in the literature. The first is control-based intervention, which aims to help individuals gain better control of the cognitive processes underlying implicit bias and to prevent the processes from affecting their decisions and behaviors. The second is augmentation-based intervention, which enhances human decision-making capacities via human-machine interactions in which a computer acts as a companion or advisor in an ongoing context-sensitive way. In what follows—and illustrating the utility of our framework—we consider these promising new changed-based, control-based, and augmentation-based interventions.[13] Moreover, we will show that by considering D1 and D2 together, we can address some worries raised in "Section 3.6" concerning the ineffectiveness of cognition-based interventions.

Advance Change-Based Interventions with Evidence-Based Approach, Personalization, and AI-Related Technology First, the recent literature on implicit bias can help advance better AI-assisted, change-based interventions. For example, research shows that only a select set of change-based interventions have robust short-term effects, e.g., competition with shifted group boundaries, shifting group affiliations under threat, etc. (Lai et al. 2016). However, none of the existing approaches take advantage of these findings. There is also a rich literature concerning ways to enhance the effectiveness of change-based interventions (Brownstein 2019). By incorporating these recent findings, we will be more likely to develop effective AI-assisted interventions.

Moreover, we can improve the effectiveness of change-based interventions by reflecting on D1 and D2 together. For example, we can maximize the potential of these various interventions by personalizing cognition-based interventions. With the help of better analytics, KBSs can identify the types of implicit bias that require the most attention—as well as the most effective interventions—for particular recruiters. For instance, KBSs may determine, with predictive analytics, that a recruiter is relatively more biased against women of color in contexts of evaluating intelligence (Madva and Brownstein 2018). KBSs may then implement the interventions to target the relevant biased associations in a more focused way. Additionally, KBSs can determine what types of change-based interventions will work better for the recruiter by running predictive analysis on the feedback collected. Such analytic information can help implement interventions that produce the most benefit with limited resources.

Third, we can also exploit new, AI-related technology and new modes of human-machine interaction to improve the interventions' effectiveness. For example, VR can (1) create a vivid and rich virtual social and physical environment for reducing biases, in which (2) the users can engage more actively in an immersive and self-directed way, in order to (3) influence multiple cognitive mechanisms (including visual, auditory, cognitive, emotional, evaluative, etc.). All of these features have been shown to promote more effective changes in one's implicit attitudes (Byrd 2019). Moreover, VR can also make interventions more fun by turning them into a VR game or other entertainment experience (e.g., using Deepfake technology to give any Hollywood

---

[13] However, we should not think of the three types of cognition-based interventions as a final and unrevisable category of cognition-based intervention. This is because as our knowledge about the mechanisms of implicit bias grows, new types of cognition-based intervention may become available.

movie an all-Asian cast to increase positive experiences with outgroup members). As the availability of VR equipment approximates smartphones, change-based interventions will no longer be restricted to lab settings. Rather, interventions can be undergone daily for an extended period. This has the potential to increase their long-term effectiveness.[14]

Facilitate Control-Based Interventions with Analytics and Automation Another example of how D2 helps explore promising AI-assisted approaches is drawing our attention to control-based interventions. Empirical research has suggested that some control-based interventions may be efficacious. Among these are implementation intentions, which are "if-then" plans that specify a response that a decision-maker can perform upon encountering a particular perceptual cue. For example, if I see a dark-skinned face, then I will respond by thinking "good" (Gollwitzer 1999). Compared with change-based approaches, control-based interventions may lead to immediate behavioral change through self-control, and there is also evidence suggesting that these interventions have long-term effects (Lai and Banaji 2019; Burns et al. 2017; Monteith et al. 2013). Research suggests, in other words, that AI-assisted control-based interventions are worth exploring.

Again, bringing D1 into consideration can be beneficial. One potential criticism of control-based interventions is that they may not be practically feasible because they may place great demands on cognitive resources—in particular, they tax an agent's scarce resources for self-control (Botvinick and Braver 2015). For example, implementation intention requires subjects to be on the lookout for the specific "if" condition and recall the relevant "then" condition to control their behavior. It thus requires considerable effort to implement just one implementation intention—much less than the number required to adequately address bias in the hiring process. AI-related technology, such as AR, can make control-based interventions more feasible by taking the cognitive burden off the users. For example, a pair of Google glasses can help detect several different "if" conditions in the environment and remind the user of the relevant "then" conditions. Moreover, better predictive analytics can further enhance the quality of interventions. A real-time prediction can help initiate the implementation intention either before or shortly after the "if" condition obtains. A faster prediction entails a more effective control-based intervention because cognitive control is most effective when control-related signals are generated early enough to have an impact upon biased decision-making. Finally, given that the large number of potential "if" conditions in the environment may still overwhelm the user despite automation, prescriptive analytics provided by KBSs can help determine which "if" conditions should be prioritized in the relevant contexts.

Note that while the above change-based and control-based interventions come with clear benefits, both require significant time and resources to train recruiters who are participating in the hiring processes (although see Madva (2017) for an argument that such commitment may not be as big as has been assumed). Besides, these interventions clearly invite ethical concerns related to privacy, as they require the collection of massive amounts of personal

---

[14] However, we need to be careful of the unforeseen ethical consequences of interventions (such as those involving VR). For example, Madary and Metzinger (2016) point out that VR can induce illusions of embodiment and change one's long-term psychological states. Risky content and privacy are critical issues too. Therefore, they offer a list of ethical recommendations as a framework for future study. While there will always be unforeseeable risks involved in new technology, such research will help us minimize it.

data (See "Section 3.2."). Additionally, as some of the control-based interventions involve manipulation without the user's consent (e.g., nudging), they can violate the user's autonomy—beyond the ethical concern of AI paternalism (see "Section 4.3" for more discussion). These drawbacks may pose an obstacle for companies or recruiters who wish to adopt this strategy to reduce bias.

Take Full Advantage of Augmentation-Based Interventions One final case illustrates the benefits of bringing together all aspects of our framework when exploring potential AI-assisted interventions. D2 draws our attention to the relative neglect of decision augmentation, a field that examines how human-machine interaction can enhance the quality of decision-making (Jarrahi 2018). Although this entire paper can be seen as an application of decision augmentation, we have not emphasized the field's key insights. To begin with, this field stresses natural human-machine interaction and hence focuses on systems that could engage with humans using natural language as well as intuitive data visualization. Also, it focuses on the complementarity between humans and machines. For instance, when tackling a problem that is difficult for humans to solve, humans may seek help from AI to analyze Big Data. AI can also provide feedback in a user-friendly form such as a narrative explanation that summarizes complex data in a narrative form. Finally, humans can ultimately accept or reject such advice after taking on board broader considerations that may be hard for AI to take on board.

For example, a social robot can work as an advisor to the recruitment team during interviews, similar to a moral advisor in the case of moral enhancement (Savulescu and Maslen 2015). It can do so by incorporating both the existing and potential interventions discussed above. For example, it can provide "translated" information about interviewees for proper contextualization (e.g., by interpreting their performance relative to their access to opportunity) at the appropriate time. Moreover, it can lead the team to engage in deliberation that is less likely to be biased (e.g., by adopting more criteria-based judgments using criteria that track actual performance). It can also bring attention to potentially biased responses in interviews. There are newer strategies that can be incorporated as well. It is possible for social robots, for example, to create a more inclusive interview environment by discouraging sexist speech with a subtle disapproving frown (Paiva et al. 2018). Moreover, the robot could also act as a "Socratic Assistant" to provide empirical support, improve conceptual clarity and argumentative logic, etc. (Lara and Deckers 2019). Of course, as augmentation-based intervention can potentially integrate all interventions discussed above, it will confront all the challenging ethical issues for each type of intervention.

In short, D2 can help us systematically explore new AI-assisted interventions by bringing together insights from newly emerging empirical research and AI-related technologies. Overall, we have shown that our framework is useful for developing new approaches for reducing the harm of implicit bias.[15]

---

[15] The interventions proposed in this paper are generally based on currently available AI and AI-related technologies; however, their advancement relies on the development of AI research in some domains. In particular, predictive interventions face the challenge of modeling and predicting the behavior of an individual accurately; on top of that, prescriptive interventions, in order to suggest decisions to its user, require a causal model, which represents how the intervention leads to results for a particular user (Albrecht and Stone 2018; Sheridan 2016). Finally, we need empirical research to validate the effectiveness of the specific implementation of these interventions.

4.3 Emerging Ethical Issues for Promising Interventions

The new approaches we discussed can remedy some of the limitations that face existing interventions, but they also raise new ethical challenges, including the difficulty of attributing individual and collective responsibility—as well as the threat to human autonomy. We will not be able to resolve these controversial issues in this paper; however, we aim to show that they are not insurmountable problems that prevent us from adopting these promising AI-assisted interventions.

First, the attribution of moral responsibility is complicated by automated decision-making by KBSs (Doshi-Velez and Kortz 2017), especially in contexts of collective decision-making involving a group of human and AI agents (Winsberg et al. 2014). To handle the issues of the attribution of individual responsibility, one promising way is to adopt ethical guidelines that require humans to be the ultimate decision-makers in decisions involving KBSs (Hung and Yen 2020). So an individual (e.g., a manager) needs to make an explicit decision to transfer some power of decision-making to KBSs, ensuring that it is human agent who is ultimately responsible for the decisions.

Moreover, Miller's (2017, 2018) account of *collective moral responsibility* can also help the attribution of collective responsibility. According to this account, agents with different *roles* in the collective decision-making process can have a collective end in a chain of responsibility (i.e., each agent makes a different and distinct contribution, according to their roles, to the collective end and shares collective responsibility). So when a recruiter makes a morally wrong decision based on a problematic recommendation by a KBS, which in turn results from the negligence of a software engineer, both the recruiter and the engineer are collectively responsible and accountable (praised or blamed) for the wrong decision.[16] In short, existing theoretical frameworks about collective responsibility can help hold the right agent responsible and accountable for the wrong decision and hence alleviate the ethical concern.

Second, as AI-assisted interventions shape human decisions through interfering with the deliberation processes, violation to human autonomy (i.e., roughly, the freedom of self-determination and self-control) can become a serious ethical concern. For example, when AI increases a human's own good at the cost of restricting autonomy, AI paternalism may happen. Likewise, nudging, which manipulates decision-making without consent or understanding on behalf of the individuals involved, may also violate their autonomy. Again, these issues are difficult but not completely unsolvable. With regard to AI paternalism, introducing the well-developed guidelines from bioethics (e.g., opting-out, informed consent, and the principle of autonomy) can be helpful. For example, the principle of autonomy could be helpful (Amnesty International UK 2018; Floridi and Cowls 2019; Anonymous, forthcoming). According to the principle, (i.e., respect for the rights of self-determination), one should determine by herself whether to exchange partial autonomy (e.g., determining which route to go) for some good (e.g., the convenience of trip planning on Google maps), thus preventing KBSs from undermining her autonomy.

---

[16] According to Miller (2018), *responsibility* is about the ability to fulfill a duty, and *accountability* is about the liability to respond to one's performance of duties. Accountability presumes responsibility, but is not identical with it. Please see Miller (2018) for further distinction of the two notions.

About the worry that nudging may violate autonomy, Barton (2013) argues that in some cases, nudging (e.g., tobacco health warnings) can in fact foster autonomy (e.g., helping smokers to control themselves better). It has also been argued by Engelen and Nys (2020) that such a worry may be overblown and should be reassessed by clarifying the notion of autonomy. According to them, nudging's threat to autonomy is rarely supported by a proper understanding of autonomy. Moreover, given a graded understanding of autonomy, nudging can restrict one's autonomy without completely violating it.[17] In short, this account helps alleviate the ethical concern of nudging, even if it does not clear it away completely. To summarize, the promising AI-assisted approaches discussed above are ethically viable ways of addressing the problem of implicit bias; however, further research into the ethical implications of these approaches still needs to be pursued.

5 Designing a Better Hiring Process with the Framework

The previous discussions have mainly focused on individual interventions, the majority of which target just one individual recruiter at a specific phase of the hiring process. However, the hiring process can involve multiple recruiters, the biases of whom can affect any phase of the recruitment process. As such, ensuring a fair hiring process means paying attention to the hiring process as a whole. This implies that intervention design should aim at providing a multi-factorial approach that combines interventions to restructure the hiring processes. Again, our framework can work as a useful conceptual tool here: it helps design interventions that work synergistically by clarifying each approach's function, its locus of intervention, as well its strengths and weaknesses.

Different approaches (AI-assisted or not) are not mutually exclusive; rather, they can often complement each other to enhance the overall efficacy of the intervention. For example, existing intervention strategies heavily rely on masking the demographic contents of resumes. While it has positively influenced the recruitment of people from certain underrepresented groups (e.g., women; Krause et al. 2012), this practice may also disadvantage candidates of lower socioeconomic status by obscuring the fact that their achievements are exemplary relative to the relatively limited opportunities they have had (see "Section 3.4"). This problem can be addressed by replacing this problematic resume screening process with a new form of low-cost interview, thus restructuring the hiring process. This lost-cost interview method reduces implicit bias by combining an input-based intervention that collects alternative data from candidates during an automated interview, with an output-based intervention that makes fully automated evaluative decisions.

It is also possible to combine control-based interventions with the practice of selectively masking applicants' demographic information. On the one hand, control-based interventions can be overwhelming if the recruiters are constantly alerted with cues for control during their decision. On the other hand, masking demographic

---

[17] Engelen and Nys (2020) propose the concept of *perimeters of autonomy*, according to which changes in an agent's options within the perimeters can occur without precluding his autonomy because he still has a range of options to choose from. Nonetheless, there may be an issue about how to draw the perimeters.

information may lead to inadequate contextualization of the applicant's behaviors and performance as discussed previously. By combining the two interventions in the hiring process, masking can reduce the frequency of cues for control (as some of the triggers for implicit bias are masked), while control-based interventions, such as implementation intention, can reduce biased decision-making based on unmasked, contextualizing, yet potentially bias-inducing information.

This design strategy has implications for research on implicit bias intervention. Implicit bias, as many scholars have emphasized, involves multiple interacting cognitive mechanisms. The strategy of combining multiple complementary interventions has the benefit of simultaneously targeting a multiplicity of underlying cognitive processes. Doing so may result in more effective and sustained changes which overcome a key problem identified by current literature: the failure of individual cognitive interventions to produce long-term effects.

6 Conclusion and Future Directions

To summarize, implicit bias is a complex problem underpinned by multiple, interacting cognitive mechanisms. We have proposed a framework to assess existing AI-assisted interventions, explore future approaches, and restructure hiring processes. We are confident that the framework can be applied to tackle implicit bias in domains other than job recruitment, such as policing and healthcare. Granted, there are unresolved limitations facing individual interventions, some of which generalize to many other AI applications—including, but not limited to, the normative issues discussed in "Section 3.2" and "Section 4.3." However, we are optimistic that future research will lead to the development of technological and social solutions that address them appropriately.

While we have focused exclusively on interventions that target cognitive mechanisms, structuralists may argue that our framework fails to address structural problems. However, recent research has stressed the dynamic interactions between cognitive and structural factors. Soon (2019), for example, has emphasized the dynamic causal processes by which biased mind and structure sustain themselves mutually. Liao and Huebner (2020) also argue that implicit bias is a multifaceted phenomenon involving dynamic interaction and mutual dependence among cognitive, social, and physical factors.[18] That is, "individualistic interventions can have structural effects, and vice versa" (Soon 2019, p. 3), and they are equally important in achieving equity (Saul 2018; Zheng 2018). For example, a cognitive intervention can draw a company's attention to low inclusivity in its policies, as well as any micro-aggressive behaviors in its workplace. This could lead to institutional change within the company, which in

---

[18] The complex interaction between cognitive and structural factors can have unpredictable consequences. It is exemplified in the change of implicit and explicit antigay bias before and after same-sex marriage legalization. Ofosu et al. (2019) found that implicit and explicit antigay bias decreased before the legalization of same-sex marriage. Nevertheless, the change of attitude following legalization differs depending on whether the legalization was passed locally: a deeper decrease was found if the legalization was passed locally, whereas an increase following federal legalization in states that never passed local legalization. However, note that Tankard and Paluck (2017) found that federal legalization led individuals to change their perceptions of social norms regarding gay marriage, but not their personal attitudes.

turn makes it more likely to adopt a more comprehensive framework of cognitive interventions. In fact, we believe, as our framework suggests, that interventions which target multiple cognitive mechanisms, and interact dynamically with the unjust social and physical environments in which they are embedded, have the most potential to affect positive individual and structural changes.

Acknowledgements For helpful discussions and feedback on earlier drafts of this work, thanks to Michael S. Brownstein, Acer Chang, Caitrin Donovan, Ivan Gonzalez-Cabrera, Julia Haas, Richard Heersmink, Bryce Huebner, Calvin Lai, Eric Schwitzgebel, Jacob Sparks, and two anonymous referees.

Funding information This work is supported in part by an Academia Sinica Fellowship to Dr. Linus Ta-Lun Huang, sponsored by Academia Sinica, Taiwan. This research is also funded in part by the Ministry of Science and Technology Taiwan to Dr. Tzu-wei Hung (MOST 107-2410-H-001-101-MY3).

References

Agan, A., & Starr, S. (2017). Ban the box, criminal records, and racial discrimination: A field experiment. *The Quarterly Journal of Economics, 133*, 191–235.
Albrecht, S. V., & Stone, P. (2018). Autonomous agents modelling other agents: A comprehensive survey and open problems. *Artificial Intelligence, 258*, 66–95. https://doi.org/10.1016/j.artint.2018.01.002.
Amnesty International United Kingdom. (2018). Trapped in the matrix: Secrecy, stigma, and bias in the Met's gangs database. https://reurl.cc/8lmnzy. .
Barton, A. (2013). How tobacco health warnings can Foster autonomy. *Public Health Ethics, 6*(2), 207–219.
Behaghel, L., Crepon, B., & Le Barbanchon, T. (2015). Unintended effects of anonymous resumes. *American Economic Journal: Applied Economics, 7*, 1–27.
Biggs, M. (2013). *Prophecy, self-fulfilling/self-defeating*. Encyclopedia of Philosophy and the Social Sciences. Inc: SAGE Publications. https://doi.org/10.4135/9781452276052.n292. isbn:9781412986892.
Botvinick, M., & Braver, T. (2015). Motivation and cognitive control. *Annual Review of Psychology, 66*(1), 83–113.
Brownstein, M. (2018). *The implicit mind: Cognitive architecture, the self, and ethics*. New York, NY: Oxford University Press.
Brownstein, M. (2019). Implicit bias. In E. Zalta (Ed.), *The Stanford Encyclopedia of Philosophy* (Fall 2019).
Burns, D., Parker, M., & Monteith, J. (2017). Self-regulation strategies for combating prejudice. In C. Sibley & F. Barlow (Eds.), *The Cambridge Handbook of the Psychology of Prejudice* (pp. 500–518).
Byrd, N. (2019). What we can (and can't) infer about implicit bias from debiasing experiments. *Synthese.*
Caliskan, A., Bryson, J. J., & Narayanan, A. (2017). Semantics derived automatically from language corpora contain human-like biases. *Science, 356*, 183–186.
Castelvecchi, D. (2016). Can we open the black box of AI? *Nature, 538*(7623), 20–23. https://doi.org/10.1038/538020a.
Chamorro-Premuzic, Tomas (2019). Will AI reduce gender bias in hiring? Harvard Business Review.
Clabaugh, C., & Matarić, M. (2018). Robots for the people, by the people. *Science Robotics, 3*(21).
Daumeyer, N. M., Onyeador, I. N., Brown, X., & Richeson, J. A. (2019). Consequences of attributing discrimination to implicit vs. explicit bias. *Journal of Experimental Social Psychology, 84*, 103812.
De Houwer, J. (2019). Implicit bias is behavior: A functional-cognitive perspective on implicit bias. *Perspectives on Psychological Science, 14*(5), 835–840.
Devine, P. G., Forscher, P. S., Austin, A. J., & Cox, W. T. (2012). Long-term reduction in implicit race bias: A prejudice habit-breaking intervention. *Journal of Experimental Social Psychology, 48*(6), 1267–1278. https://doi.org/10.1016/j.jesp.2012.06.003.
Doshi-Velez, F., & Kortz, M. (2017). Accountability of AI under the law: The role of explanation. In *Berkman Klein center working group on explanation and the law*. Berkman Klein: Center for Internet & Society working paper.
Dunham, C. R., & Leupold, C. (2020). Third generation discrimination: An empirical analysis of judicial decision making in gender discrimination litigation. *DePaul J. for Soc. Just, 13.*
Eightfold AI. (n.d.). Talent Diversity. Retrieved from https://reurl.cc/EKp05m

Engelen, B., & Nys, T. (2020). Nudging and autonomy: Analyzing and alleviating the worries. *Review of Philosophy and Psychology, 11*(1), 137–156.

Entelo. (n.d.). Entelo Platform Reports. Retrieved from https://reurl.cc/Gko62y

Equal Reality. (n.d.). Retrieved from https://equalreality.com/index

FitzGerald, C., Martin, A., Berner, D., & Hurst, S. (2019). Interventions designed to reduce implicit prejudices and implicit stereotypes in real world contexts: A systematic review. *BMC Psychology, 7*(1), 29. https://doi.org/10.1186/s40359-019-0299-7.

Floridi, L. (2015). *The ethics of information*. Oxford University Press.

Floridi, L., & Cowls, J. (2019). A unified framework of five principles for AI in society. *Harvard Data Science Review*.

Foley, M., & Williamson, S. (2018). Does anonymising job applications reduce gender bias? Understanding managers' perspectives. *Gender in Management, 33*(8), 623–635. https://doi.org/10.1108/GM-03-2018-0037.

Forscher, P. S., Mitamura, C., Dix, E. L., Cox, W. T., & Devine, P. G. (2017). Breaking the prejudice habit: Mechanisms, timecourse, and longevity. *Journal of Experimental Social Psychology, 72*, 133–146.

Forscher, P. S., Lai, C. K., Axt, J. R., Ebersole, C. R., Herman, M., Devine, P. G., & Nosek, B. A. (2019). A meta-analysis of change in implicit bias. *Journal of Personality and Social Psychology, 117*, 522–559.

Galinsky, A. D., & Moskowitz, G. B. (2000). Perspective-taking: Decreasing stereotype expression, stereotype accessibility, and in-group favoritism. *Journal of Personality and Social Psychology, 78*(4), 708.

Garcia, M. (2016). Racist in the machine: The disturbing implications of algorithmic bias. *World Policy Journal, 33*(4), 111–117.

Gollwitzer, P. M. (1999). Implementation intentions: Strong effects of simple plans. *American Psychologist, 54*(7), 493–503. https://doi.org/10.1037/0003-066X.54.7.493.

Hajian, S., Bonchi, F., & Castillo, C. (2016). Algorithmic bias: From discrimination discovery to fairness-aware data mining. In *Proceedings of the 22nd ACM SIGKDD international conference on knowledge discovery and data mining* (pp. 2125-2126).

Haslanger, S. (2012). *Resisting reality*. Oxford: OUP.

HireVue. (2019). CodeVue offers powerful new anti-cheating capability in coding assessment tests. Retrieved from https://reurl.cc/24D9An

HireVue. (n.d.). HireVue video interviewing software. Retrieved from https://reurl.cc/NapMKk

Hiscox, M. J., Oliver, T., Ridgway, M., Arcos-Holzinger, L., Warren, A., & Willis, A. (2017). Going blind to see more clearly: Unconscious bias in Australian public service shortlisting processes. *Behavioural Economics Team of the Australian Government*. https://doi.org/10.1016/j.jmrt.2015.05.003.

Hodson, G., Dovidio, F., & Gaertner, L. (2002). Processes in racial discrimination. *Personality and Social Psychology Bulletin, 28*(4), 460–471.

Holpuch, A., & Solon, O. (2018, May 1). Can VR teach us how to deal with sexual harassment? In *The Guardian* Retrieved from https://reurl.cc/A1KreQ.

Holroyd, J., & Sweetman, J. (2016). The heterogeneity of implicit biases. In M. Brownstein & J. Saul (Eds.), *Implicit Bias and philosophy, volume 1: Metaphysics and epistemology*. Oxford University Press.

Huebner, B. (2016). Implicit bias, reinforcement learning, and scaffolded moral cognition. In M. Brownstein & J. Saul (Eds.), *Implicit bias and philosophy* (Vol. 1). Oxford: Oxford University Press.

Human Rights Watch. (2019). *World report, 2019* https://reurl.cc/6g641d. .

Hung, T.-w. (2020). A preliminary study of normative issues of AI prediction. *EurAmerica, 50*(2), 205–227.

Hung, T.-w. & Yen, Chun-pin (2020). On the person-based predictive policing of AI. *Ethics and Information Technology*. https://doi.org/10.1007/s10676-020-09539-x.

IBM Knowledge Center (n.d.). Retrieved from https://reurl.cc/W4k9DO

IEEE Global Initiative. (2016). *Ethically aligned design. IEEE Standards*, v1.

Interviewing.io. (n.d.) Retrieved from https://interviewing.io/

Jarrahi, M. (2018). Artificial intelligence and the future of work. *Business Horizons, 61*(4), 577–586.

Krause, A., Rinne, U., & Zimmermann, K. (2012). Anonymous job applications in Europe. *IZA Journal of European Labor Studies, 1*(1), 5.

Lai, C. K., & Banaji, M. (2019). The psychology of implicit intergroup bias and the prospect of change. In D. Allen & R. Somanathan (Eds.), *Difference without domination: Pursuing justice in diverse democracies*. Chicago, IL: University of Chicago Press.

Lai, C. K., Marini, M., Lehr, A., Cerruti, C., Shin, L., Joy-Gaba, A., et al. (2014). Reducing implicit racial preferences I. *Journal of Experimental Psychology: General, 143*(4), 1765.

Lai, C. K., Skinner, L., Cooley, E., Murrar, S., Brauer, M., Devos, T., et al. (2016). Reducing implicit racial preferences II. *Journal of Experimental Psychology: General, 145*(8), 1001.

Lara, F., & Deckers, J. (2019). Artificial intelligence as a Socratic assistant for moral enhancement. *Neuroethics*. https://doi.org/10.1007/s12152-019-09401-y.

Liao, S., & Huebner, B. (2020). Oppressive Things. Philosophy and Phenomenological Research. https://doi.org/10.1111/phpr.12701.

Lu, J., & Li, D. (2012). Bias correction in a small sample from big data. *IEEE Transactions on Knowledge and Data Engineering, 25*(11), 2658–2663.

MacDorman, K. F., & Chattopadhyay, D. (2016). Reducing consistency in human realism increases the uncanny valley effect; increasing category uncertainty does not. *Cognition., 146*, 190–205.

Machery, E. (2016). De-freuding implicit attitudes. In M. Brownstein & J. Saul (Eds.), *Implicit bias and philosophy, Metaphysics and epistemology* (Vol. 1, pp. 104–129). Oxford: Oxford University Press.

Madary, M. & Metzinger, T.K. (2016). Real virtuality: A code of ethical conduct. Recommendations for good scientific practice and the consumers of VR-technology. *Front. Robot. AI* 3:3. https://doi.org/10.3389/frobt.2016.00003.

Madva, A. (2017). Biased against debiasing: On the role of (institutionally sponsored) self-transformation in the struggle against prejudice. *Ergo, 4*.

Madva, A., & Brownstein, M. (2018). Stereotypes, prejudice, and the taxonomy of the implicit social mind. *Noûs, 52*(3), 611–644.

Miller, S. (2017). Institutional responsibility. In M. Jankovic & K. Ludwig (Eds.), *The Routledge handbook of collective intentionality* (pp. 338–348). New York: Routledge.

Miller, S. (2018). *Dual use science and technology, ethics and weapons of mass destruction*. Springer.

Monteith, J., Woodcock, A., & Lybarger, E. (2013). *Automaticity and control in stereotyping and prejudice*. Oxford: OUP.

Mori, M. (1970/2012). The uncanny valley (K. F. MacDorman & N. Kageki, trans.). IEEE Robotics and Automation, 19(2), 98–100. https://doi.org/10.1109/MRA.2012.2192811.

Mya. (n.d.). Meet Mya. Retrieved from https://mya.com/meetmya

Obermeyer, Z., Powers, B., Vogeli, C., & Mullainathan, S. (2019). Dissecting racial bias in an algorithm used to manage the health of populations. *Science, 366*(6464), 447–453. https://doi.org/10.1126/science.aax2342.

Ofosu, E. K., Chambers, M. K., Chen, J. M., & Hehman, E. (2019). Same-sex marriage legalization associated with reduced implicit and explicit antigay bias. *Proceedings of the National Academy of Sciences, 116*, 8846-8851.

Paiva, A., Santos, P., & Santos, F. (2018). Engineering pro-sociality with autonomous agents. *Proc of AAAI*.

Peck, T., Seinfeld, S., Aglioti, S., & Slater, M. (2013). Putting yourself in the skin of a black avatar reduces implicit racial bias. *Consciousness and Cognition, 22*(3), 779–787.

Pymetrics. (n.d.). Retrieved from https://www.pymetrics.com/

Régner, I., Thinus-Blanc, C., Netter, A., Schmader, T., & Huguet, P. (2019). Committees with implicit biases promote fewer women when they do not believe gender bias exists. *Nature Human Behaviour*, 1–9.

Richardson, R., Schultz, J., & Crawford, K. (2019). Dirty data, bad predictions: How civil rights violations impact police data, predictive policing systems, and justice. *New York University Law Review, 94*, 192–233.

Samek, W., Wiegand, T., & Muller, K.-R. (2017). Explainable artificial intelligence: Understanding, visualizing and interpreting deep learning models. *ITU journal: ICT Discoveries, 1*.

Saul, J. (2018). Should we tell implicit bias stories? *Disputatio., 10*(50), 217–244.

Savulescu, J., & Maslen, H. (2015). Moral enhancement and artificial intelligence. *Beyond Artificial Intelligence* (pp. 79–95). In J. Romportl, E. Zackova, J. Kelemen (eds), Beyond artificial intelligence. Springer.

Schwitzgebel, E. (2013). A dispositional approach to attitudes: Thinking outside of the belief box. In N. Nottelmann (Ed.), *New essays on belief*. New York: Palgrave Macmillan.

Seibt, J., & Vestergaard, C. (2018). Fair proxy communication. *Research Ideas and Outcomes, 4*, e31827.

Sharda, R., Delen, D., & Turban, E. (2020). *Analytics, data science, & artificial intelligence: Systems for decision support*. Pearson.

Sheridan, T. B. (2016). Human–robot interaction. *Human Factors: The Journal of the Human Factors and Ergonomics Society, 58*(4), 525–532. https://doi.org/10.1177/0018720816644364.

Skewes, J., Amodio, D., & Seibt, J. (2019). Social robotics and the modulation of social perception and bias. *Philosophical Transactions of the Royal Society B, 374*(1771).

Snyder, M., Tanke, E. D., & Berscheid, E. (1977). Social perception and interpersonal behavior: On the self-fulfilling nature of social stereotypes. *Journal of Personality and Social Psychology, 35*, 655–666.

Soon, V. (2019). Implicit bias and social schema. *Philosophical Studies*, 1–21.

Sue, D., Capodilupo, C., Torino, G., Bucceri, J., Holder, A., Nadal, K., & Esquilin, M. (2007). Racial microaggressions in everyday life. *American Psychologist, 62*(4), 271.
Suresh, H., & Guttag, J. V. (2019). A framework for understanding unintended consequences of machine learning. *arXiv* preprint arXiv:1901.10002.
Surowiecki, J. (2005) *The wisdom of crowds*. New York, NY: Anchor Books.
Sweeney, L. (2013). Discrimination in online ad delivery. *Queue, 11*(3).
Taddeo, M. (2019). Three ethical challenges of applications of artificial intelligence in cybersecurity. *Minds and Machines, 29*(2), 187–191.
Taddeo, M., & Floridi, L. (2018). How AI can be a force for good. *Science, 361*(6404), 751–752.
Tankard, M. E., & Paluck, E. L. (2017). The effect of a supreme court decision regarding gay marriage on social norms and personal attitudes. *Psychological Science, 28*, 1334–1344.
Textio. (n.d.). Textio hire. Retrieved from https://textio.com/products/
Unbias.io. (n.d.) Retrieved from https://unbias.io/
Vantage Point. (n.d.). Retrieved from https://www.tryvantagepoint.com/
Wachter, S., Mittelstadt, B., & Floridi, L. (2017). Transparent, explainable, and accountable AI for robotics.
Winsberg, E., Huebner, B., & Kukla, R. (2014). Accountability and values in radically collaborative research. *Studies in History and Philosophy of Science Part A, 46*, 16–23.
Zaleski, Katharine. (2016). Virtual reality could be a solution to sexism in tech. Retrieved from https://reurl.cc/vnezZk
Zheng, R. (2018). Bias, structure, and injustice: A reply to Haslanger. *Feminist Philosophy Quarterly, 4*(1).

Publisher's Note Springer Nature remains neutral with regard to jurisdictional claims in published maps and institutional affiliations.

Affiliations

Ying-Tung Lin[1] · Tzu-Wei Hung[2] · Linus Ta-Lun Huang[2,3]

[1] Institute of Philosophy of Mind and Cognition, National Yang-Ming University, No.155, Sec.2, Linong Street, Taipei 112, Taiwan

[2] Institute of European and American Studies, Academia Sinica, No. 128, Sec. 2, Academia Rd., Nankang District, Taipei 115, Taiwan

[3] Department of Philosophy, University of California, 9500 Gilman Drive # 0119, La Jolla, San Diego, CA 92093-0119, USA

Philosophy & Technology (2021) 34 (Suppl 1):S91–S104
https://doi.org/10.1007/s13347-020-00403-w

COMMENTARY

Beyond a Human Rights-Based Approach to AI Governance: Promise, Pitfalls, Plea

Nathalie A. Smuha[1]

Received: 23 January 2020 / Accepted: 22 April 2020 / Published online: 24 May 2020
© Springer Nature B.V. 2020

Abstract

This paper discusses the establishment of a governance framework to secure the development and deployment of "good AI", and describes the quest for a morally objective compass to steer it. Asserting that human rights can provide such compass, this paper first examines what a human rights-based approach to AI governance entails, and sets out the promise it propagates. Subsequently, it examines the pitfalls associated with human rights, particularly focusing on the criticism that these rights may be too Western, too individualistic, too narrow in scope and too abstract to form the basis of sound AI governance. After rebutting these reproaches, a plea is made to move beyond the calls for a human rights-based approach, and start taking the necessary steps to attain its realisation. It is argued that, without elucidating the applicability and enforceability of human rights in the context of AI; adopting legal rules that concretise those rights where appropriate; enhancing existing enforcement mechanisms and securing an underlying societal infrastructure that enables human rights in the first place, any human rights-based governance framework for AI risks falling short of its purpose.

Keywords Artificial intelligence · Ethics · Human rights · AI governance · AI for good

1 The Quest for "Good AI"

Artificial intelligence ("AI")-systems[1] are currently enjoying a summer to envy. After having gone through a few tough winters, they secured not only renewed attention from

---

Chapter 6 was originally published as Smuha, N. A. Philosophy & Technology (2021) 34 (Suppl 1):S91–S104. https://doi.org/10.1007/s13347-020-00403-w.

[1] For a definition of AI or AI-systems as used throughout this article, reference can be made to the definition formulated by the European Commission's High-Level Expert Group on AI (AI HLEG 2019a), published simultaneously with its Ethics Guidelines for Trustworthy AI (AI HLEG 2019b).

✉ Nathalie A. Smuha
nathalie.smuha@kuleuven.be

[1] Department of International & European Law, Faculty of Law, KU Leuven, Tiensestraat 41, 3000 Leuven, Belgium

experts and laypersons alike, but also unprecedented levels of funding (Bernal 2019). This is much thanks to research breakthroughs in the field of machine learning, as well as the availability of big data and large computing power at a lower cost. Yet the summer also brought forth renewed attention to the socio-economic implications of these systems, including their potential to generate economic and societal benefits on the one hand, and their ability to cause significant harm on the other. As a consequence, two trends can be observed.

The first is a focus on AI-systems' beneficial *use* and aims to incentivise socially beneficial applications, thus allowing the benefits of AI-systems to flow to humanity as a whole rather than only to those already enjoying a large concentration of money or power. Examples thereof are AI-applications that help in reducing humans' negative impact on the environment, that render the provision of healthcare more accessible or that more generally contribute to the achievement of the UN Sustainable Development Goals (Vinuesa et al. 2020). This trend is increasingly denoted as fostering "AI for (Social) Good" (Cowls et al. 2019).[2]

The second trend is a focus on AI-systems' beneficial *development* and stems from the growing insight that technologies—including AI-systems—are not neutral (MacKenzie and Wajcman 1985). The manner in which AI-systems are designed, their models developed, their performance tested or their data selected, has a direct impact on the systems' decision-making process and—in turn—on their outcomes. Consequently, a growing number of initiatives have been set up to ensure that system developers take such impact into account from the design phase onwards, by identifying and specifying the ethical values they wish to protect and by embedding these into the AI-systems' architecture. This trend is also referred to as ensuring AI-systems that are "ethical by-design" (Dignum et al. 2018).

Both trends are, of course, heavily intertwined. Not much social good will be generated by an AI-system that was developed without considering ethical values in its design phase (for instance by foregoing to tackle its potential for biased decision-making or its vulnerability to harmful adversarial attacks). Conversely, an AI-system that embeds ethical values in its design could still be used in applications that are detrimental to the social good or that focus solely on the good of one individual or group at the cost of others. Yet both nevertheless raise an important definitional question that needs to be addressed by those aspiring to work towards their achievement: what is this "good" that AI-systems should be steered towards or their design should be aligned with?[3]

The quest for a definition of "the good" is as ancient as the history of philosophy and, until today, remains a challenging one. Throughout the ages, philosophers have formulated a wide variety of definitions, as well as moral theories underpinning these definitions. A moral relativist would thus hold that what is considered to be "good"—or "good AI"—depends on the time, culture, societal background and personal views of the person whose opinion is asked. Hence, what a Belgian human rights lawyer might consider a good AI-application could be held in a very different esteem by a North-Korean teacher, a Saudi-Arabian law enforcer, a German industrialist, an American lobbyist—or even simply a Belgian corporate lawyer. Moreover, each of them could

---
[2] Sometimes also referred to as "AI for common good" (e.g. Beerendt 2019).
[3] Throughout this paper, reference to "good AI" encompasses both of the aims mentioned above, i.e. ensuring that AI-systems are "ethical-by-design" and steering their them towards "AI for (Social) Good".

rely on different well-established theories to underpin their arguments on why a certain AI-application may or may not be "good".

To the extent that those different individuals are interested in purchasing an AI-system for personal use, this diversity of views does not necessarily raise an issue.[4] Each will simply make their own purchasing choice in accordance with their idea of what a "good" application entails (and in accordance with the size of their wallet). However, when it comes to the public governance of AI-systems, a relativistic view of this diversity does pose a challenge. How should those in charge of creating governance policies decide which norms to consider when aspiring to steer AI-systems towards good designs and uses?

To start with, they would much rather befriend a moral objectivist who—contrary to the relativist—would hold that there is something that can objectively be considered to be "good", regardless of societal context or personal view. While moral objectivists would not necessarily agree on what a "good" AI-system consists of, they would at least be able to reassure regulators that there are some values out there that can be considered "good" universally, and that these are the ones that should be striven towards. Such reassurance is especially helpful for regulators who need to devise governance measures that tackle the ethical risks of AI-systems for Belgians and Germans—or for Belgians and Americans—alike. Given that those risks do not stop at the national or even the European border, a universally acceptable moral compass for an AI governance framework is most useful. The question then remains, what is that compass?

This is precisely the question that also the European Commission, *the* regulatory actor[5] at EU level, grappled with when drafting its European strategy on artificial intelligence (European Commission 2018), wishing to steer its policies (and EU public funding) towards "good AI". In the context of its strategy, the Commission set up an independent High-Level Expert Group on Artificial Intelligence. The Group was tasked with the drafting of two documents: Ethics Guidelines for AI ("Guidelines"), addressed primarily to those developing and deploying the technology, and AI policy and investment recommendations ("Recommendations"), addressed primarily to regulators such as the European Commission and EU member states. A diversity of views was aspired by appointing experts from different countries, backgrounds and interest groups, with the purpose to move beyond such diversity and reach—to the extent possible—some consensus on the ethical challenges raised by AI-systems (Smuha 2019). After almost a year of deliberations and a public consultation, in April 2019, the Guidelines were published and its seven key requirements for "Trustworthy AI" (their conceptualisation of "good AI") blessed by the European Commission (2019). The Group's approach to overcome ethical relativism consisted of identifying those values that come closest to something moral objectivists and relativists alike should be able to agree on: human rights.

2 The Promise

According to the Guidelines (AI HLEG 2019b), "*respect for fundamental rights, within a framework of democracy and the rule of law, provides the most promising*

---

[4] Assuming, of course, that these applications for personal use do not create adverse impacts upon third parties—which is not a given.
[5] Throughout this paper, the term "regulator" is used broadly, denoting entities able to create both policies and legally binding or non-binding regulation.

foundations for identifying abstract ethical principles and values, which can be operationalised in the context of AI." The quest for a normative framework to guide both the development and use of AI-systems towards "the good" thus resulted in identifying human rights—or fundamental rights as they are called in Europe—as the foundation thereof.

The Guidelines start by specifying human rights' dual role within the framework of "Trustworthy AI", which the Group characterised as AI-systems that are (1) legal, (2) ethical and (3) robust, and the foundational ambition to be striven towards. Where human rights are understood as legally enforceable rights—such as those enshrined in the Charter of Fundamental Rights of the European Union ("EU Charter") or in other binding legislation—they fall under the first component of Trustworthy AI (legal AI). Yet the fact that human rights are also bestowed on individuals by mere virtue of their status as human beings, regardless of any legal enforceability, also renders them part of Trustworthy AI's second component (ethical AI). While not explicitly stated in the Guidelines, it could furthermore be argued that ensuring AI-systems' robustness also contributes to securing the physical and mental integrity of individuals interacting therewith (the right of which is enshrined in Article 3 of the EU Charter), and that human rights might hence also overlap with the third component of Trustworthy AI (robust AI).

The Guidelines subsequently set out how, based on five "families" of human rights,[6] four abstract ethical principles are derived.[7] On that basis—one level of concreteness further—seven essential requirements for Trustworthy AI are identified.[8] To operationalise the Guidelines' framework and ensure that its guidance can be applied in practice, the last part of the document consists of an Assessment List for AI developers and deployers.[9] Given the importance of human rights within the Guidelines' framework, it is no coincidence that the Assessment List's first requirement entails an evaluation of the AI-system's potential negative impact on human rights.

This importance was echoed in the Group's second deliverable. Whereas the Guidelines focused solely on ensuring ethical and robust AI, the Recommendations (AI HLEG 2019c) put forward concrete suggestions for regulators on adopting binding legislation to advance Trustworthy AI's third component, legal AI. Across these recommendations, the need to protect human rights is equally stressed. For instance, for any AI-system with the potential to interfere with an individual's human rights, the Recommendations require regulators to consider introducing inter alia a mandatory obligation to conduct a "Trustworthy AI assessment" (p40), akin and complementary to

---

[6] These families broadly correspond to the categories of rights that can be found in the EU Charter as follows: (1) respect for human dignity, (2) freedom of the individual, (3) respect for democracy, justice and the rule of law, (4) equality, non-discrimination and solidarity and (5) citizens' rights.
[7] These principles are (1) respect for human autonomy, (2) prevention of harm, (3) fairness and (4) explicability.
[8] The seven requirements comprise the securement of (1) human agency and oversight, (2) technical robustness and safety, (3) privacy and data governance, (4) transparency, (5) diversity, non-discrimination and fairness, (6) societal and environmental wellbeing and (7) accountability.
[9] After the publication of the Guidelines' first draft in December 2018, a public consultation was organised to gather stakeholder feedback, which was subsequently incorporated in the Guidelines' version of April 2019. Between June and December 2019, the Guidelines' third chapter—the Assessment List—underwent a more focused consultation in the form of a "piloting phase", whereby organisations were asked to pilot the List and feedback was sought specifically on its relevance and operationability in different use cases. The feedback gathered through this second consultation will result in a revised version of the Assessment List in 2020.

the more established "data protection impact assessment".[10] Such assessment should include a human rights impact assessment that also ensures specific attention to AI-systems' impact on the rights of children, the rights of individuals in relation to the state, and the rights of persons with disabilities. Furthermore, for AI-systems entailing such risk, the Recommendations also raise the need to introduce mandatory traceability, auditability and ex-ante oversight requirements; a stakeholder consultation and the obligation to ensure appropriate (by default and by design) procedures for redress in case of mistakes, harms or infringement of other rights. The necessity to safeguard human rights within the context of AI-systems is repeated throughout the document in numerous other recommendations and can hence be seen as a red thread in both of the Group's (complementary) deliverables.

Whilst the choice for a human rights-based approach to AI governance is neither very surprising nor unique to the Commission's expert group (see also, e.g. Amnesty International and Access Now 2018; Latonero 2019; Yeung et al. 2019; McGregor et al. 2019; Council of Europe 2019), the reasons behind the choice remain interesting to examine. Given the "EU" context of the drafting exercise (the European Commission being the instigator of the Guidelines), the attribution of a special role for human rights is merely logical. Respect for such rights forms an inherent part of the European constitutional landscape and is firmly enshrined in Article 2 of the *Treaty on European Union* as a foundational Union value. The EU Charter further fortified the position that human rights enjoy in the EU legal order, and stressed the importance they carry not only across EU institutions but also in member states' legal systems whenever they implement EU law (de Mol 2016).

Yet, more importantly, the rights considered to be fundamental in the EU are widely accepted also far beyond the EU. In other words, they are considered universal, both because they are universally recognised by virtually each country in the world and because they are universally applicable to all human beings regardless of any individual trait. In addition, the existence of a larger institutional framework around human rights at national, international and supranational level, including established institutions such as agencies and courts with the specific purpose to enforce those rights, enshrines their standing within the global order (Yeung et al. 2019). Therefore, human rights can serve as that much sought-after morally objective compass towards securing "good AI". As concerns their *design*, developers and deployers of AI-systems should ensure that the values embedded in and protected by human rights, from human dignity to non-discrimination, are safeguarded throughout the systems' entire lifecycle. As concerns their *use*, the aim of *AI for (Social) Good* can likewise be oriented through human rights' normative framework. Indeed, in some situations, AI-systems can not only safeguard but also enable and enhance human rights, and these applications should be particularly incentivised. It is, moreover, important to stress not only the safeguarding role that human rights can play against AI-systems' adverse impacts but also their ability to support the development and uptake of those systems through enabling rights such as, for instance the right to scientific research and the freedom to conduct a business—likewise protected by the EU Charter.

The status of human rights as universal is however not uncontested, and the same goes for their aptitude to constitute a foundational framework for ensuring "good AI".

---

[10] See article 35 of the General Data Protection Regulation.

Human rights have, for instance, been branded as too Western, too individualistic, too narrow in scope and too abstract to be helpful in this regard. But does such criticism hold? If we aspire to use a human rights-based approach to secure a governance framework for "good AI", some of the common objections against human rights merit an examination.

3 The Pitfalls

3.1 Too Western?

A first and often-uttered criticism against human rights is that their claim to universality is nothing more than a bias towards Western values (Panikkar 1982; Talbott 2005; Le 2016). Considered to be originating from the West, they are branded by some as a feature of Western imperialism or continued colonialism, imposing cultural hegemony where instead a pluralism of cultural values exists that is not adequately reflected in contemporary human rights documents. There are a number of ways to rebut such branding (Huber 2014; Shaheed and Richter 2018). These include enumerating the list of non-Western countries that signed the original Universal Declaration of Human Rights, conceiving them as a diplomatically achieved result of international negotiation amongst states rather than the expression of a philosophical theory, pointing out the significant similarities between regional human rights instruments throughout the world or raising the universal nature of human rights organisations actively monitoring and investigating the (sadly likewise universal) infringement thereof.

However, even if we were to concede that in the past they were not—or today they are not—universal, one could still plausibly argue that, regardless thereof, they *ought* to be universal. Moving to the *ought* realm requires a normative justification, but one that is abundantly found in human rights theories (e.g. Rawls 1999; Hayden 2001; Griffin 2008; Gilabert 2018). In other words, the promise brought by a human rights-based framework need not fall or stand with its actual universality. Similarly, the argument that human rights are continuously infringed and hence ineffective (Posner 2014) does not diminish the moral guidance they can nevertheless offer for any governance framework. Rather, such argument may—rightfully—drive us to reconsider their existing monitoring and enforcement mechanisms and examine how we can adapt those to better safeguard human rights (see infra).

3.2 Too Individualistic?

If not too Western, are human rights too individualistic?[11] Human rights express the idea that each individual is absolute, unique and inherently deserving of protection, typically grounding this characterisation upon the notion of human dignity (e.g. in the EU Charter, but also elsewhere, see Luban 2015; Gilabert 2018). The strong emphasis on the individual's dignity and hence on individuality is at times perceived as creating an opposition between the interests of the individual (protected by human rights) and

---

[11] Individualism as an ideology is strongly associated with Western thought, hence to a certain extent linking this second reproach of human rights with the first.

the interests of the state or society at large (against which individuals are protected by virtue of human rights). Undoubtedly, the interests of individuals and of society are not always aligned and, in certain situations, prioritising the protection of a single person's rights might occur at the cost of societal benefits (Tharoor 1999). Such tension might for instance arise between an individual's right to protect her medical data on the one hand and the potential to use that data—together with the data of many others—to advance AI-systems that can more accurately identify diseases and appropriate medical treatments (Taddeo 2016). A similar juxtaposition can arise between the interests of individuals and the environment, which—depending on the (time) perspective one takes—will not always be aligned either. Consequently, perceiving human rights as primarily focused on individuals might give rise to the claim that they are inadequate to deal with the tensions arising from these conflicting interests, and by extension inadequate to fulfil a purposeful role within a society that also embraces communitarian and environmental values.

Such reading of human rights first of all disregards the various social rights that are part of human rights legislation, such as the right to education, housing or healthcare. Second, it ignores the fact that also the more "individual" rights have a social raison d'être. Indeed, societies in which individuals have a private space to think, act and speak foster not only individual but also societal benefits. Protecting these rights within a given society hence enhances not only the "good" of the specific rights-bearer, but the welfare of all. It is therefore no surprise that human rights are also increasingly used to seek redress against various environmental harms, as it is not a far stretch to argue that a clean and healthy environment is a prerequisite to enjoy many of these rights (Knox 2013).

Third, such reading overlooks the fact that human rights are not absolute.[12] The EU Charter for instance carefully lays down the conditions under which the rights recognised therein can be limited: (1) the limitation must be provided for by law, (2) it must respect the essence of the right in question and (3) subject to the principle of proportionality must be necessary and genuinely meet objectives of general interest recognised by the Union or the need to protect the rights and freedoms of others (Article 52). Conceptually similar formulations can be found in the European Convention of Human Rights (under each article enshrining a right), and in the Universal Declaration of Human Rights (Article 29). In other words, human rights-based frameworks specifically recognise that enforcing the rights of one might hamper the rights of others and that those different interests need to be balanced. This balancing exercise occurs not only between the different individual and societal interests that can be at stake but also between the different rights that can be applicable and potentially conflicting in a given context. It is precisely the task of those enforcing human rights to ensure that justice is done by reaching the appropriate equilibrium of those rights for the specific situation.

Furthermore, to do so, enforcers can draw on previously undertaken balancing exercises, which advance predictability and legal certainty. Indeed, decades of institutionalised human rights enforcement resulted in a rich jurisprudence that can also guide enforcers when dealing with the impact of AI-systems on individuals and

---

[12] Only few exceptions exist, such as the right to human dignity, the right not to be subjected to slavery, torture, and cruel, inhumane or degrading treatment or punishment (though for the latter, see also Greer 2015).

society and with the tensions stemming therefrom—be it in terms of conflicting rights, principles or interests. While these tensions cannot simply be dissolved, the frameworks' strength lies in the fact that it allows them to be acknowledged, made explicit, rationally reflected upon in a manner tailored to the specific context, as well as rendered challengeable. If we wish to advance a governance framework that enables "good AI"—and that allows us to face the difficult but inevitable question of who the beneficiaries of that "good" should be—those are precisely the steps to secure.

3.3 Too Narrow?

Another possible objection concerns human rights' narrow scope. Traditionally, human rights only apply in a vertical, but not in a horizontal setting. Individuals can raise a human rights claim against the state, but not against another private party, be it an individual or a company (Knox 2008). And to the extent that many (if not most) AI-systems are developed and deployed by private companies rather than by the state, this might render the human rights framework less relevant, or even inapplicable, since a potentially harmed individual cannot directly rely thereon against an AI-system's private producer. For several reasons, however, this objection should not be seen as an obstacle to rely on human rights for an appropriate AI governance framework.

First, some of the most problematic uses of AI-systems concern applications deployed by the state while exercising important public functions, such as the application of automated facial recognition by police forces, or the deployment of predictive AI-systems within the judiciary. These contexts are particularly sensitive in light of the government's monopoly of the legitimate use of physical force. It is hence crucial that the deployment of AI-systems by the government—regardless of whether those systems were developed by a public or private party—is subject to enforceable human rights legislation. In this regard, it can be noted that states can also play a catalysing role to foster human rights-compliant AI, by ensuring that (private) developers of AI-systems meet human rights standards regardless of whether these systems are ultimately deployed in a public or private context.

Second, even to the extent that human rights are primarily creating obligations towards states rather than private entities, it is still the responsibility of states to ensure that, within their jurisdictions, individuals can enjoy these rights without any interference—including from private parties. Hence, if states do their job, human rights at the very least create indirect duties upon private actors, which also comprise those developing and deploying AI-systems.

Third, the traditional non-horizontality of human rights is increasingly placed under pressure and slowly but surely eroding. An increasing number of cases are witnessed whereby human rights were (successfully) relied upon against corporations, e.g. by applying a broad reading of the notion of "state" or by invoking customary international law (Baughen 2015). Furthermore, recent case law of the European Court of Justice has clarified that the EU Charter—for which a vertical scope was specifically delineated in Article 51—can also have a horizontal dimension. After a long series of cases which left the matter open, the Court's Grand Chamber's judgement in *Bauer* et al. (Joined Cases C-569/16 and C-570/16) found that human rights which are mandatory in nature and comply with all other conditions of direct effect of EU law (their formulation being clear, precise and unconditional) can be directly invoked before a national or EU court, regardless of whether the dispute arises between an individual and a state or between two private parties (Frantziou 2018).

Notwithstanding the above, even if a specific human right could not be directly invoked against a private party (or could not be invoked at all, for instance if it concerns a jurisdiction that lacks the legal enforceability thereof), this would still not diminish the role that it can play to secure an appropriate AI governance framework. Even non-enforceable human rights can still inform and inspire the creation of legally enforceable regulation to safeguard individuals against AI-systems' adverse impacts or to steer their application towards the good.

3.4 Too Abstract?

Human rights are able to provide protection in a diversity of situations, much thanks to their abstract formulation. By applying and interpreting them in light of the specific case where their need for protection arises, they remain relevant also in previously non-encountered circumstances. Human rights' abstract formulation also allows for their tailored interpretation within diverse social and cultural contexts.[13] However, the possibility of those different interpretations—including interpretations that offer uneven levels of protection—also points to the disadvantage of their broad nature, and raises the question whether human rights are too abstract to be meaningful. If everything hinges on a specific interpretation in a given case, how then can human rights enforcers guarantee an adequate standard of protection?

This issue is not unique to human rights, but befalls all norms that correspond to a "principle" rather than a "rule", a difference conceptualised most notably by Ronald Dworkin (1977). Although Dworkin's conceptualisation was (at least in part) devised to rebut the legal positivistic view of the law, most legal positivists today would agree that the legal system not only comprises but also requires both rules and principles (Utz 1992).[14] While the strength of one can be seen as the weakness of the other (from overly broad and flexible to overly descriptive and rigid), rules and principles operate in complementary ways.

Generally speaking, principles—including most, if not all, formulations of human rights—are more abstract than rules, and intended to be malleable to an infinite number of situations. They provide an overarching norm arguing in one direction and requiring contextual interpretation, without necessitating a particular decision. Conversely, rules prescribe more concretely the legal consequences that follow in a given situation, and hence typically limit the potential for significantly differing interpretations. Especially when considering law from a naturalistic point of view, most rules can be understood as a concretisation of one or more principles (Verheij et al. 1998). This concretisation occurs particularly where over time, for instance through continuous legal practice, a

---

[13] Both the European Court of Human Rights (Tsarapatsanis 2015) and—in a more subtle manner—the Court of Justice of the European Union (Gerard 2011), at times make use of this feature when they defer a right's interpretation (and the question of a potential infringement) to the state itself so as to accommodate cultural differences in its concretisation. It should, however, be noted that the doctrine of the "margin of appreciation" has not been spared from criticism. Opponents accuse it to open the gate towards a weakening or under enforcement of human rights, while proponents claim that such deference does not undermine the right as such, but rather ensures that the right's interpretation is uttered by those most capable of doing so in the given context.

[14] Note, however, that the characteristic distinction between principles and rules is not always strict (see also Soeteman 1991).

specific interpretation of a principle is consolidated into a rule. Subsequently, but not necessarily, this interpretation might then be codified into a legal instrument. Although not all principles are concretised through prescriptive rules, many—including human rights—eventually or partially are. A well known example hereof is the European fundamental right to personal data protection (enshrined in Article 8 of the EU Charter), which has been concretised through inter alia[15] the General Data Protection Regulation.

Consequently, if a specific human right is deemed too abstract to provide a sufficiently clear or uniform interpretation to protect against AI's adverse impacts, the desired interpretation of a concretisation of that right—by establishing a (legislative) rule—is always an option. It is hence up to regulators, together with all stakeholders involved, to identify areas in which human rights' abstract nature offers a welcome adaptability to the novel issues raised by AI-systems, and areas in which it instead raises too much uncertainty or imprecision to provide adequate protection. And while some human rights will fall under the former category and others under the latter, the relevance of neither is diminished. Both provide relevant principles that need to be applied to a given situation and that can morally guide the development and use of AI-systems—whether through a codified ruled or an ad hoc interpretation.

4 The Plea

Although human rights are not bulletproof, they provide a sound normative framework to steer AI-systems towards the good. Rather than getting distracted by the criticism raised above and losing our way amidst ethical relativism, human rights' position to underlie, guide and fortify a governance framework for AI should be irrefutably recognised. Whilst there is hence no need to entirely reinvent the wheel when devising a governance framework for AI, it would equally be a mistake to think that the work ends there. Reaching consensus on the fact that AI governance must be grounded in human rights is only a very first step. It provides a blueprint, but not an actual AI governance framework. A plea is therefore made to move beyond the cry for a human rights-based approach and start securing the essential constituents that such framework implores. Four are highlighted in particular.

First, an intensive knowledge enhancement process must take place. In one direction, those developing and deploying AI-systems need to gain an understanding of the values that human rights protect, the applicability—and potential legal enforceability—of those rights regarding their own actions, and the manner in which they can be practically implemented. AI practitioners—especially those with a non-legal background—still too rarely have human rights on their radar. Lacking knowledge of what these rights entail, they fail to apprehend the relevance thereof to their own domain. This attitude is, however, naïve at best and dangerous at worst. Even when leaving out of consideration their aim to intentionally misuse AI-systems, the risk still remains for these systems to infringe human rights in entirely unintentional ways, or to be acquired by third parties who do have the aim to cause intentional infringements.

---

[15] Besides the GDPR, other pieces of legislation likewise concretise the fundamental right to personal data protection, at EU level (for instance the Data Protection Law Enforcement Directive 2016/680 of 27 April 2016) or at national level.

Although various initiatives, including the Ethics Guidelines for Trustworthy AI, have the explicit objective to raise awareness about these risks, more work is still to be done.

In the other direction, it is equally crucial that those in charge of enforcing human rights gain an understanding of how AI-systems work, and the manner in which their particular design, training or deployment might breach human rights. Whilst, today, judges already have the ability to apply human rights legislation to breaches thereof through AI-systems, and right-bearers already have the ability to contest those breaches, both must first understand the underlying logic of the systems—and of the systems' deployers—to grasp how a breach of such right might manifests itself within this context, and what the legal consequences would entail. It is hence not necessary to wait for new human rights-inspired legislation to arrive before starting to enforce human rights in an AI-context, especially as the process to adopt such legislation may take a long time. Yet in order to enforce them, one must first be aware of their applicability.

Second, given that human rights consist of principles that must be interpreted in a given context, their scope of protection strongly depends upon the interpretation granted to them by various actors, be it ex ante (e.g. organisations setting up compliance processes) or ex post (e.g. judges analysing human rights claims). A continuous assessment is hence needed of the current interpretations given to these principles, the ways in which these interpretations might fall short to provide satisfying protection against the novel issues raised by AI-systems, and the areas in which the introduction of new—more concretising—rules might advance this goal. Evidently, this assessment cannot be made by one actor alone. Besides the involvement of regulators, judges, practitioners and experts of various relevant disciplines, a wide public debate is necessary to attain informed and democratically legitimised decisions on the manner in which those more concrete rules should be shaped.

Third, besides focusing on the substantive scope of human rights protection, a thorough evaluation is needed of their current enforcement mechanisms. None of the novel issues raised by AI-systems will make human rights obsolete. And while their adverse impacts might manifest themselves in novel ways (e.g. discrimination based on new or unforeseen characteristics), the principles that human rights protect (e.g. non-discrimination) will remain relevant regardless of technological progress. However, these novel manifestations are nevertheless significantly challenging the enforcement of both human rights and the rules that concretise them. The effectiveness of these mechanisms must hence be assessed specifically within the context of AI-systems and the challenges that those systems imply. The scope of this assessment should not be limited to the potential necessity of introducing enhanced enforcement tools. It should also consider the introduction of new rules that—rather than setting out new substantive norms—create new procedural norms to advance the enforcement of existing principles. For instance, if an endemic deficiency of transparency—not just of the AI-system but of the human decisions surrounding the system (which data was selected, which optimisation criteria where chosen, which testing method was deployed)—renders it impossible to ascertain whether a substantive human right (e.g. non-discrimination) was breached to begin with, the allocation of more resources for enforcers or the establishment of a new right to non-discrimination will not do. Instead, one might consider introducing new procedural rules for high-risk applications (e.g. mandatory documentation or auditability obligations) that will enable the enforcement of already applicable substantive rules. This consideration was also recognised in the European Commission's White Paper on AI, which provides a first sketch of what such obligations could look like (European Commission 2020).

Finally, the enjoyment of human rights falls or stands with the values of the underlying societal infrastructure. If the necessary building blocks that enable human rights in society are not secured, none of the abovementioned steps matter. The revival of populism throughout the world—including in EU member states—is accompanied by a weakening of democracy, the rule of law and the independence of the judiciary, and is threatening corollary values like freedom, equality, justice and peace. AI-systems, as well as numerous other tools, can be used to put these values further under pressure, for instance by targeting democratic institutions and decision-making processes. However, the achievability of any human rights-based governance framework and its protection hinges upon these essential values. When working towards such governance framework for AI, it is therefore primordial to likewise consider the necessity to secure an underlying societal infrastructure that enables human rights in the first place.

5 Conclusion

While the quest to define "good AI" is relatively new, the quest to define the "good" is not and over the ages resulted in a plethora of ethical theories. Those preferring to leave moral relativism aside have not been discouraged thereby and continued their search for a morally objective compass to guide a governance framework for AI. Against the background of increasing concern for the adverse impacts that AI-systems might generate, that search recently intensified as numerous organisations started putting forward ethical guidelines to steer AI towards the good (Jobin et al. 2019). This article has argued that human rights can function as that much sought-after moral compass to constitute the basis of an AI governance framework. Although, amongst other re-proaches, human rights have been criticised for being too Western, too individualistic, too narrow and too abstract, they gained a quasi-constitutional status within the European Union and are recognised as essential normative values throughout the world. More than providing a mere ethical stance, human rights also contain safeguarding and enabling legal obligations that are already enforceable today, also in the context of AI.

Human rights are, however, not flawless. They are only as helpful as their notoriety. They are only as protective as their interpretation. They are only as strong as their enforcement mechanisms. And they are only as robust as their underlying societal infra-structure. Consequently, besides setting out the promise that a human rights-based approach to AI governance entails and refuting its pitfalls, this article has made the plea to move beyond this debate and start taking the necessary steps to secure such governance frame-work in practice. Ensuring "good AI"—however one defines it—is not a static goal. It is a dynamic and iterative process, and the more we learn about the technology and its impact on us, the more its achievement will be approached. However, it is clear that—beyond an increase in resources and skills for enforcers—this process will require (1) a translation exercise that illuminates the applicability and vulnerability of human rights in the context of AI, (2) the adoption of new legislation that concretises human rights wherever their interpretation is too abstract to provide sufficient protection or their legal enforceability is desired but lacking, (3) a thorough evaluation of the current enforcement mechanisms of these rights and (4) the realisation that all human rights, legal rules and governance frameworks—whichever their scope—are dependent on the underlying societal infrastruc-ture of which they are part. Ensuring a society in which the enablers of human rights' enjoyment— such as democracy, the rule of law and the independence of the judiciary—are protected (whether threatened by the use of AI-systems or by other means) is therefore equally critical. Ultimately, securing "good AI" starts with securing a "good society".

Funding Information Nathalie Smuha's work is supported by the Flanders Research Foundation (FWO).

References

Amnesty International & Access Now. (2018). The Toronto Declaration: Protecting the rights to equality and non-discrimination in machine learning Systems, https://www.accessnow.org/the-toronto-declaration-protecting-the-rights-to-equality-and-non-discrimination-in-machine-learning-systems/ . Accessed 20 May 2020.
Baughen, S. (2015). Customary international law and its horizontal effect? Human rights litigation between non-state actors. *Rutgers University Law Review, 67*(1), 89–126.
Beerendt, B. (2019). AI for the common good?! Pitfalls, challenges and ethics pen-testing. *Paladyn, Journal of Behavioral Robotics, 10*, 44–65.
Bernal, N. (2019). AI investment reaches record levels in the UK. The Telegraph, https://www.telegraph.co.uk/technology/2019/09/09/ai-investment-reaches-record-levels-uk/ . Accessed 20 May 2020.
Council of Europe. (2019), Mandate of the Ad Hoc Committee on Artificial Intelligence (CAHAI), CM/Del/Dec(2019)1353/1.5, https://search.coe.int/cm/Pages/result_details.aspx?ObjectId=09000016809737a1 . Accessed 20 May 2020.
Cowls, J., King, T., Taddeo, M. and Floridi, L. (2019). Designing AI for Social Good: Seven Essential Factors, available at *SSRN*: https://ssrn.com/abstract=3388669.
de Mol, M. (2016). Article 51 of the charter in the legislative processes of the member states. *Maastricht Journal of European and Comparative Law, 23*(4), 640–666.
Dignum, V., Baldoni, M., Baroglio, C., Caon, M., Chatila, R., Dennis, L., Genova, G., Kliess, M., Lopez-Sanchez, M., Micalizio, R., Pavon, J., Slavkovik, M., Smakman, M., van Steenbergen, M., Tedeschi, S., van der Torre, L., Villata, S., de Wildt, T., and Haim, G. (2018). Ethics by design: Necessity or curse? In proceedings of the 1st international conference on AI ethics and society, ACM, 60–66.
Dworkin, R. (1977). *Taking rights seriously*. Cambridge: Harvard University Press.
European Commission (2018). Artificial Intelligence for Europe. *Communication*, Brussels, 25.4.2018, COM(2018) 237 final.
European Commission (2019). Building Trust for Human-Centric AI. *Communication*, Brussels, 8.4.2019, COM(2019) 168 final.
European Commission (2020). White paper on Artificial Intelligence – A European approach to excellence and trust. White Paper, Brussels, 19.2.2020, COM(2020) 65 final.
Frantziou, E. (2018), Joined cases C-569/16 and C-570/16 Bauer et al: (most of) the charter of fundamental rights is horizontally applicable. *Euroepanlawblog*, https://europeanlawblog.eu/2018/11/19/joined-cases-c-569-16-and-c-570-16-bauer-et-al-most-of-the-charter-of-fundamental-rights-is-horizontally-applicable/. Accessed 20 May 2020
Gerard, J. (2011). Pluralism, deference and the margin of appreciation doctrine. *European Law Journal, 17*(1), 80–120.
Gilabert, P. (2018). *Human dignity and human rights*. Oxford: Oxford University Press.
Greer, S. (2015). Is the prohibition against torture, cruel, inhuman and degrading treatment really 'absolute' in international human rights law? *Human Rights Law Review, 15*(1), 101–137.
Griffin, J. (2008). *On human rights*. Oxford: Oxford University Press.
Hayden, P. (2001). *The Philosophy of Human Rights*. St. Paul, MN: Paragon Press.
High-Level Expert Group on AI (AI HLEG). (2019a). A definition of AI – Main Capabilities and Disciplines. April 2019, https://ec.europa.eu/digital-single-market/en/news/definition-artificial-intelligence-main-capabilities-and-scientific-disciplines . Accessed 20 May 2020.
High-Level Expert Group on AI (AI HLEG). (2019b). Ethics guidelines for trustworthy AI. April 2019, https://ec.europa.eu/digital-single-market/en/news/ethics-guidelines-trustworthy-ai . Accessed 20 May 2020.

High-Level Expert Group on AI (AI HLEG) (2019c). Policy and investment recommendations for trustworthy AI. May 2019, https://ec.europa.eu/digital-single-market/en/news/policy-and-investment-recommendations-trustworthy-artificial-intelligence . Accessed 20 May 2020.

Huber, W. (2014). Human rights and globalisation – are human rights a 'Western' concept or a universalistic principle? *NGTT DEEL, 55*(1), 117–137.

Jobin, A., Ienca, M., & Vayena, E. (2019). The global landscape of AI ethics guidelines. *Nat Mach Intell, 1,* 389–399.

Knox, J. (2008). Horizontal human rights law. *American Journal of International Law, 102*(1), 1–47.

Knox, J. (2013). Report of the independent expert on the issue of human rights obligations relating to the enjoyment of a safe, clean, healthy and sustainable environment. United Nations General Assembly, https://www.ohchr.org/EN/HRBodies/HRC/RegularSessions/Session25/Documents/A-HRC-25-53_en.doc . Accessed 20 May 2020.

Latonero, M. (2019). Governing artificial intelligence: Upholding human rights and human dignity. *Data & Society,* https://datasociety.net/wp-content/uploads/2018/10/DataSociety_Governing_Artificial_Intelligence_Upholding_Human_Rights.pdf . Accessed 20 May 2020.

Le, N. (2016). Are human rights universal or culturally relative? *Peace Review, 28*(2), 203–211.

Luban, D. (2015), Human rights pragmatism and human dignity. In Cruft, R., Liao; S. and Renzo M. (eds.), Philosophical Foundations of Human Rights, Oxford: Oxford University Press.

MacKenzie, D., & Wajcman, J. (1985). *The social shaping of technology: how the refrigerator got its hum.* Milton Keynes: Open University Press.

McGregor, L., Murray, D., & Ng, V. (2019). International human rights law as a framework for algorithmic accountability. *ICLQ, 68*(2), 309–343.

Panikkar, R. (1982). Is the notion of human rights a Western concept? *Diogenes, 30*(120), 75–102.

Posner, E. (2014). The case against human rights. *The Guardian,* https://www.theguardian.com/news/2014/dec/04/-sp-case-against-human-rights . Accessed 20 May 2020.

Rawls, J. (1999). *The law of peoples.* Cambridge, MA: Harvard University Press.

Shaheed, A. and Richter, R. (2018). Is 'human rights' a Western concept?, *IPI Global Observatory,* https://theglobalobservatory.org/2018/10/are-human-rights-a-western-concept/ . Accessed 20 May 2020.

Smuha, N. (2019). The EU approach to ethics guidelines for trustworthy artificial intelligence. *Computer Law Review International, 20*(4), 97–106.

Soeteman, A. (1991). *Hercules aan het werk* (pp. 41–56). Rechtsbeginselen Ars Aequi: Over de rol van rechtsbeginselen in het recht.

Taddeo, M. (2016). Data philanthropy and the design of the infraethics for information societies. *Philosophical Transactions of the Royal Society A, 374.* https://doi.org/10.1098/rsta.2016.0113.

Talbott, W. (2005). *Which rights should be universal?* Oxford: Oxford University Press.

Tharoor, S. (1999). Are human rights universal? *World Policy Journal, 16*(4), 1–6.

Tsarapatsanis, D. (2015). The margin of appreciation doctrine: A low-level institutional view. *Legal Studies, 35*(4), 675–697.

Utz, S. (1992). Rules, principles, algorithms and the description of legal systems. *Ratio Juris., 5*(1), 23–45.

Verheij, B., Hage, J., & Van Den Herik, J. H. (1998). An integrated view on rules and principles. *Artificial Intelligence and Law, 6*(1), 3–26.

Vinuesa, R., Azizpour, H., Leite, I., Balaam, M., Dignum, V., Domisch, S., Felländer, A., Langhans, S. D., Tegmark, M., & Fuso Nerini, F. (2020). The role of artificial intelligence in achieving the sustainable development goals. *Nature Communications, 11*(233), 1–10.

Yeung, K., Howes, A., & Pogrebna, G. (2019). AI governance by human rights-Centred design, deliberation and oversight: An end to ethics washing. In M. Dubber & F. Pasquale (Eds.), *The Oxford Handbook of AI Ethics* (forthcoming). Oxford: Oxford University Press.

Publisher's Note Springer Nature remains neutral with regard to jurisdictional claims in published maps and institutional affiliations.

Philosophy & Technology (2021) 34 (Suppl 1):S105–S109
https://doi.org/10.1007/s13347-020-00409-4

COMMENTARY

Testing the Black Box: Institutional Investors, Risk Disclosure, and Ethical AI

Trooper Sanders[1] 📵

Received: 25 February 2020 / Accepted: 11 June 2020 / Published online: 24 July 2020
© The Author(s) 2020

Abstract

The integration of artificial intelligence (AI) throughout the economy makes the ethical risks it poses a mainstream concern beyond technology circles. Building on their growing role bringing greater transparency to climate risk, institutional investors can play a constructive role in advancing the responsible evolution of AI by demanding more rigorous analysis and disclosure of ethical risks.

Keywords Artificial intelligence · Black box · Investors · AI ethics · Pension funds

In its most recent public filings to the United States Securities and Exchange Commission (SEC), Microsoft Corporation (2020) alerted investors to risks from its growing artificial intelligence business. The company's September 2019 10-Q filing warned: "AI algorithms may be flawed. Datasets may be insufficient or contain biased information. Inappropriate or controversial data practices by Microsoft or others could impair the acceptance of AI solutions.... Some AI scenarios present ethical issues. If we enable or offer AI solutions that are controversial because of their impact on human rights, privacy, employment, or other social issues, we may experience brand or reputational harm" (2019). These disclosures mark a meaningful step forward in bringing AI ethics from the academy and advocacy and into the mainstream of the marketplace. And while flagging risks to investors is not the same as the market rewarding companies for the ethical quality of their development, application, and commercialization of AI, it can help make emerging technologies and business practices powered by AI more accountable to investors and the public.

Since 2005, the SEC has required companies issuing shares to the public to disclose risks (Election Code of Federal Regulation 2020). Firms must "disclose material factors that may adversely affect the issuers business, operations, industry or financial position, or its future firm performance" (Filzen, McBrayer, and Shannon, 2016). For example, a pharmaceutical

---

Chapter 7 was originally published as Sanders, T. Philosophy & Technology (2021) 34 (Suppl 1):S105–S109. https://doi.org/10.1007/s13347-020-00409-4.

Trooper Sanders is a former Rockefeller Foundation Fellow.

✉ Trooper Sanders
tsanders@wisewhisper.com

[1] Rockefeller Foundation, New York USA

company's filing might discuss growing competition from generic drug manufacturers while a financial services firm might discuss the impact of regulatory changes and associated costs on the business. Access to good information is an essential part of efficient markets. In economics, the ideal state is when consumers and producers have perfect knowledge about price, quality, and other factors affecting decision-making. While individual investors have access to considerable information, it is institutional investors, the investment funds, insurance companies, and pension funds with more than $100 trillion under management globally, who have the means to track, analyze, and react to the vast quantity of data available today (Segal 2018). A study by finance professors Field and Lowry (2005) found that institutional investors make better use of publicly available information than individual investors (2006).

In theory, greater transparency about risks should improve investors' situational awareness and their ability to make sound decisions but in practice disclosures often fall short of the mark. An analysis by the Investor Responsibility Research Center Institute said that risk factor disclosures by large companies "do not provide clear, concise and insightful information…are not tailored to the specific company…[and] tend to represent a listing of generic risks, with little to help investors distinguish between the relative importance of each risk to the company" (2020). Indeed, one of Microsoft's leading competitors in AI summed up their risk factors in their quarterly filing crisply: "Our operations and financial results are subject to various risks and uncertainties…which could adversely affect our business, financial condition, results of operations, cash flows, and the trading price of our common and capital stock" (Alphabet Inc, 2019).

However imperfect, institutional investors can use their influence to bring greater transparency to AI in two ways: pushing regulators to demand more disclosure by public companies and assessing the ethical AI fitness of companies in their portfolio who have materially significant stakes as AI developers or consumers. The evolving role of institutional investors in climate change is instructive. First, climate risk is a core business concern for funds. "The prices of the assets we buy as an investor, and the degree to which these prices reflect climate risk, affect the fund's financial risk," noted Norway's Government Pension Fund, a climate risk hawk among large funds (Olsen and Grande 2019). In addition, strong corporate performance on climate change is often an indicator of shareholder-friendly efficiency and sound management and governance.

In 2007, American and European investors managing $1.5 trillion in assets joined a coalition calling on the SEC to require companies to assess and publicly disclose their financial risk related to climate change. "Climate change can affect corporate performance in ways ranging from physical damage to facilities and increased costs of regulatory compliance, to opportunities in global markets for climate-friendly products or services that emit little or no global warming pollution," the coalition argued. "Those risks fall squarely into the category of material information that companies must disclose under existing law to give shareholders a full and fair picture of corporate performance and operations" (Environmental Defense Fund 2007).

A few years later, several of the world's largest funds began to formally factor environmental, social, and governance (ESG) matters in some investment decisions. While ESG investing has its limitations for both institutional investors (OECD 2017) and for tackling the relevant concerns (Rennison 2019), it has become an important vehicle to put capital behind business practices aligned with the public interest (Eccles 2019). In addition, loose principles in the early years of ESG have evolved into more robust metrics and standards (Edgecliffe-Johnson, Nauman, and Tett 2020). For example, powerful investors, including billionaire Michael Bloomberg, and others recently kicked off an effort examining the physical, liability, and transition risks of climate change as part of establishing voluntary climate-related financial risk disclosure standards (Task Force on Climate-related Financial Disclosures 2020).

Institutional investors did not wait for climate law and regulation to settle and scale before seizing opportunities and asserting influence. A combination of hard law and regulation, non-legislative soft law, and climate ethics shaped by evolving consumer sentiment, political consensus, and social norms provided sufficient guidance and grounding. Similarly, the emerging consensus in AI ethics around transparency, justice and fairness, non-maleficence, responsibility, and privacy can provide a guidon to investors addressing AI concerns (Jobin, Inca, and Vayena 2019). Indeed, as scholars such as Gary Marchant have noted, the slow pace of legal and regulatory change in technology matters has created a void best filled by soft law tools such as professional guidelines, private standards, codes of conduct, and best practice (2019). Indeed, as key players in the economy, institutional investors could give the ethical AI field some essential oomph. As leading AI ethicist, Virginia Dignum notes: "Engineers are those that ultimately will implement AI to meet ethical principles and human values, but it is policy makers, regulators and society in general that can set and enforce the purpose" (2019).

Consider emotion recognition services that use algorithms to analyze facial features and make inferences about mood and behavior (Jee 2019). This growing segment of the AI market, worth more than $20 billion and put to use in areas ranging from workplace hiring to law enforcement, poses several ethical challenges including:

- weak scientific foundations, with one recent review of more than 1000 scientific papers finding very little evidence that facial expressions alone can predict how someone is feeling (Chen 2019);
- concerns that racial and gender bias will exacerbate existing disparities (Rhue 2019); and
- it replaces human judgment and being used without appropriate human oversight (Qumodo Ltd. 2019).

For firms offering such services, material concerns that could fall under risk disclosure requirements include:

- biased data and shaky science undermining the quality of and confidence in products leading to declining sales and market share;
- controversial applications affecting public interest concerns such as employment discrimination and abusive policing leading to greater regulatory and public relations costs; and
- the confluence of business headwinds, public resistance, and technical vulnerabilities eroding market confidence and triggering a long winter or collapse of the sector.

Customers of these services face their own risks worthy of disclosure. They include:

- harmful AI infecting the quality and reputation of core products and services leading to increased litigation risk, declining sales and market share, and unexpected mitigation costs;
- damage to the corporate brand, including its brand valuation juices share price, and relationship with customers, stakeholders, and the public; and
- productivity loss from toxic AI polluting critical operations such as talent management or a negative experience in one application of AI slowing or stopping other AI efforts that offer material benefits.

Just as changes in climate change thinking and analytics moved influential market players to act, the evolving state of the art in AI ethics can help institutional investors probe beyond disclosures in public filings (Moss 2019). First, strong ethical AI performance can be an indicator for a strong and well-managed enterprise generally, and weak performance a warning sign for more fundamental challenges that could hurt shareholders. Furthermore, the well-established body of knowledge about algorithmic bias gives analysts a strong foundation to test the material ethical risks of companies buying and selling machine learning products and services in areas as diverse as human resources, health care, and consumer banking (Raghavan et al., 2019). Companies forthcoming about the limitations of training data, bias in services and products, and steps they are taking to mitigate harm are more likely to pose fewer risks while those denying data vulnerabilities or ethical soft spots should be viewed skeptically. Investors will be able to develop deeper layers of inquiry on risk, financial performance, and other priorities as the fairness, accountability, and transparency field expands beyond technical matters such as explainability and interpretability to include rigorous treatment of the real world use and the social and organizational impact of AI (Sendak et al., 2020). In addition, greater scrutiny given to the limits of AI in sensitive sectors such as health care can help investors avoid exposure to overblown claims that harm people, damage companies, and destroy shareholder value (Szabo 2019).

In sum, while institutional investors' involvement in AI ethics is no balm to the havoc rogue AI can cause, they can be constructive allies in the push to align the power of technology and the public interest. Whether putting money behind ethical performance yields returns that sustain their interest depends on pressure from and decisions by developers, regulators, and consumers who drive AI's course.

Open Access This article is licensed under a Creative Commons Attribution 4.0 International License, which permits use, sharing, adaptation, distribution and reproduction in any medium or format, as long as you give appropriate credit to the original author(s) and the source, provide a link to the Creative Commons licence, and indicate if changes were made. The images or other third party material in this article are included in the article's Creative Commons licence, unless indicated otherwise in a credit line to the material. If material is not included in the article's Creative Commons licence and your intended use is not permitted by statutory regulation or exceeds the permitted use, you will need to obtain permission directly from the copyright holder. To view a copy of this licence, visit http://creativecommons.org/licenses/by/4.0/.

References

Alphabet Inc. (2019). Form 10-Q for the quarterly period ended September 30, 2019. https://abc.xyz/investor/static/pdf/20191028_alphabet_10Q.pdf?cache=376def7.

Chen, A. (2019). Computers can't tell if you're happy when you smile. MIT Technology Review. https://www.technologyreview.com/s/614015/emotion-recognition-technology-artifical-intelligence-inaccurate-psychology/.

Dignum, V. (2019). AI ethical principles are for us. Medium. . https://medium.com/@virginiadignum/ai-ethical-principles-are-for-us-def54e64d9a8.

Eccles, R. (2019). Why it's time to finally worry about ESG. *Harvard Business Review*. https://hbr.org/podcast/2019/05/why-its-time-to-finally-worry-about-esg.

Edgecliffe-Johnson, A., Nauman, B., and Tett, G. (2020). Davos 2020: companies sign up to environmental disclosure scheme. Financial Times. https://hbr.org/podcast/2019/05/why-its-time-to-finally-worry-about-esg.

Electronic Code of Federal Regulations (2020), Title 17: commodity and securities exchanges §229.105 (Item 105) risk factors. Current as of January 16, 2020. https://www.ecfr.gov/cgi-bin/text-idx?amp;node=17:3.0.1.1.11&rgn=div5#_top.

Environmental Defense Fund. (2007). *Major investors*. Environmental Groups Petition SEC to Require Full Corporate Climate Risk Disclosure: State Officials. https://www.edf.org/news/major-investors-state-officials-environmental-groups-petition-sec-require-full-corporate-climat.

Field, L., and Lowry, M. (2005). Institutional versus individual investment in Ipos: the importance of firm fundamentals. AFA 2006 Boston Meeting Paper. https://papers.ssrn.com/sol3/papers.cfm?abstract_id=613563.

Filzen, J., McBrayer, G., and Shannon, K. (2016). Risk factor disclosures: do managers and markets speak the same language?. **Accessed January 8, 2020**, https://www.sec.gov/comments/s7-06-16/s70616-369.pdf.

Investor Responsibility Research Center Institute (2020). "The corporate risk factor disclosure landscape," 21 and 3. **Accessed January 8, 2020**, https://www.weinberg.udel.edu/IIRCiResearchDocuments/2016/01/FINAL-EY-Risk-Disclosure-Study.pdf.

Jee, C. (2019). Emotion recognition technology should be banned, says an AI research institute. *MIT Technology Review*, https://www.technologyreview.com/f/614932/emotion-recognition-technology-should-be-banned-says-ai-research-institute/.

Jobin, A., Jenca, M., & Vayena, E. (2019). The global landscape of AI ethics guidelines. *Nature Machine Intelligence, 1*, 389–399 https://www.nature.com/articles/s42256-019-0088-2.

Marchant, G. (2019). ""Soft Law" governance of artificial intelligence," *AI Pulse*. . https://aipulse.org/soft-law-governance-of-artificial-intelligence/.

Microsoft Corporation (2020). Form 10-Q for the quarter ended September 30, 2019. . https://c.s-microsoft.com/en-us/CMSFiles/MSFT_FY20Q1_10Q.docx?version=a8248fdc-67a9-45da-1db8-818e9e8abdc9.

Moss, E. (2019). Unpacking "Ethical AI". *Points Data & Society*. https://points.datasociety.net/unpacking-ethical-ai-b770b964c236.

OECD (2017). Investment governance and the integration of environmental, social, and governance factors. https://www.oecd.org/cgfi/Investment-Governance-Integration-ESG-Factors.pdf.

Olsen, O., and Grande, Trond G. (2019). Government pension fund global account of work on climate risk. **Letter sent to the Ministry of Finance**. . https://www.nbim.no/en/publications/submissions-to-ministry/2019/government-pension-fund-global%2D%2Daccount-of-work-on-climate-risk/.

Qumodo (2019). Automatic facial recognition: why do we need a human in the loop? https://medium.com/@1530019197930/automatic-facial-recognition-why-do-we-need-a-human-in-the-loop-de8366d10680.

Raghavan, M., Barocas, S., Kleinberg, J., and Levy, K. (2019) Mitigating bias in algorithmic hiring: evaluating claims and practices. Accessed January 12, 2020. arXiv:1906.09208v3, **accessed January 10, 2020**, https://arxiv.org/pdf/1906.09208.pdf.

Rennison, J. (2019). ESG investing is a term that is too often misused. *Financial Times*. https://www.ft.com/content/ac10773a-a975-11e9-b6ee-3cdf3174eb89.

Rhue, L. (2019). Understanding the hidden bias in emotion-reading AIs. *MIT Technology Review*. . https://www.technologyreview.com/s/614015/emotion-recognition-technology-artifical-intelligence-inaccurate-psychology/.

Segal, J. (2018). The asset management industry is getting more concentrated. *Institutional Investor*. . https://www.institutionalinvestor.com/article/b1bk8n82qcc0kt/The-Asset-Management-Industry-Is-Getting-More-Concentrated.

Sendak, M., et al. (2020). The human body is a black box: supporting clinical decision-making with machine learning. arXiv:1911.08089. . https://arxiv.org/abs/1911.08089.

Szabo, L. (2019). A reality check on artificial intelligence: are health care claims overblow?. *Kaiser Health News*. . https://khn.org/news/a-reality-check-on-artificial-intelligence-are-health-care-claims-overblown/.

Task Force on Climate-related Financial Disclosures. Task force overview. Accessed January 6, 2020. https://www.fsb-tcfd.org/about/.

Publisher's Note   Springer Nature remains neutral with regard to jurisdictional claims in published maps and institutional affiliations.

Philosophy & Technology (2021) 34 (Suppl 1):S111–S123
https://doi.org/10.1007/s13347-020-00424-5

COMMENTARY

How to Handle Armed Conflict Data in a Real-World Scenario?

Anusua Trivedi[1] ⓘ **· Kate Keator[2] · Michael Scholtens[2] · Brandon Haigood[2] · Rahul Dodhia[1] · Juan Lavista Ferres[1] · Ria Sankar[1] · Avirishu Verma[1]**

Received: 30 September 2019 / Accepted: 17 August 2020 / Published online: 8 September 2020
© Springer Nature B.V. 2020

Abstract

Conflict resolution practitioners consistently struggle with access to structured armed conflict data, a dataset already rife with uncertainty, inconsistency, and politicization. Due to the lack of a standardized approach to collating conflict data, publicly available armed conflict datasets often require manipulation depending upon the needs of end users. Transformation of armed conflict data tends to be a manual, time-consuming task that nonprofits with limited budgets struggle to keep up with. In this paper, we explore the use of a deep natural language processing (NLP) model to aid the transformation of armed conflict data for conflict analysis. Our model drastically reduces the time spent on manual data transformations and improves armed conflict event classification by identifying multiple incidence types. This minimizes the human supervision cost and allows nonprofits to access a broader range of conflict data sources to reduce reporting bias. Thus, our model contributes to the incorporation of technology in the peace building and conflict resolution sector.

Keywords Armed conflict · NLP · Deep learning

1 Conflict Resolution and the Digital Age

Rather than discussing the intangible idea of using AI in peacemaking, the authors will discuss a project currently underway. On a frequent basis, social science majors with a deep understanding of structural violence or the role identity plays in peacebuilding efforts must make ethical decisions on data. In the nonprofit realm, employees often must wear many hats and in today's digital world, one of these hats

---

Chapter 8 was originally published as Trivedi, A., Keator, K., Scholtens, M., Haigood, B., Dodhia, R., Ferres, J. L., Sankar, R. & Verma, A. Philosophy & Technology 34 (Suppl 1):S111–S123. https://doi.org/10.1007/s13347-020-00424-5.

Anusua Trivedi and Kate Keator contribute equally as first authors.

✉ Anusua Trivedi
antriv@microsoft.com

Extended author information available on the last page of the article.

Reprinted from the journal

now include data guru or at least some form of data literacy. Yet how do you collect and structure information from something as messy as conflict? What are the decisions that a peacebuilder must make on a recurring basis that shape that information into something coherent and consistent? These analytical choices ranging from where to collect conflict data to what terminology to use impact the resulting analysis—a reality that peacebuilders are still grappling to understand. Just as information and communication technologies (ICTs) have changed the way people interact with each other (online chat rooms, Reddit, Facebook, Twitter etc.), ICTs have also changed how conflict resolution actors conduct conflict analysis and stakeholder mapping (Tufekci and Wilson 2012). The Syrian conflict has been one of the first major conflicts to unfold fully online. The unprecedented role digital information and communication technologies such as Twitter, Facebook, YouTube, and Reddit have had on the development of the conflict and methods to mitigate it have prompted a reexamination of how data and digital tools can support conflict resolution practitioners. As recognized by the United Nation's recently published Digital Mediation Toolkit (UN-Peacemaker 2019), the human-intensive endeavor of mediating armed conflicts is increasingly relying on digital technologies and the data from them to conduct its work. While this has not resulted in a comprehensive alteration of mediators' work, it has significantly expanded the capability of mediators to understand the complex nature of a conflict and interact with parties in a conflict. Organizations such as the Carter Center and the Armed Conflict Location and Event Data (ACLED) use publicly available information shared by social media and online news sources to document conflict activity in support of conflict resolution actors, humanitarians, and researchers. Yet the classification of conflict data is highly contextual, let alone political, with organizations classifying conflict data according to their own needs. In addition, conflict data collection is often a largely manual task due to the ubiquitous terms defining conflict. Analysts often must make subjective decisions such as what constitutes an armed clash versus mutual shelling, or what differentiates an insurgent from a rebel, or which violent and non-violent incidences to collect. This combined with the deluge of information can make the conflict data collection difficult to keep up with. Due to this information overflow, many practitioners and academics working with conflict data often turn to resources such as the Armed Conflict Location and Event Data (ACLED) Project (Raleigh et al. 2010) as a data source due to its public availability and structured datasets (ACLED 2019), even though its terminology or collection methodology may not align with a team's particular needs. Consequently, some teams spend hours manually transforming conflict data to fit their needs, thereby reducing time spent on analysis and other important tasks. According to research from the Peace Research Institute Oslo (Dupuy and Rustad 2018), interstate conflict has gradually declined in the post-Cold War era while intrastate conflict is on the rise, many of which involve contribution of troops from external states. These internationalized conflicts are on average more violent, more difficult to solve, and tend to last longer as exemplified by the ongoing Syrian conflict. Such realities require conflict resolution practitioners to find ways to handle the inevitable data overload and complexity if they are to leverage the opportunities of our digital world.

2 Data Predicament and AI

Unlike the neatly structured data sets often seen in the for-profit world—buying trends for consumer goods or quarterly sales report for a fast food chain—conflict data is often messy and inconsistent. Assigning structure requires an acknowledgement of the choices an analyst is making, ranging from what constitutes a violent incident to which term to describe a conflict actor (jihadis, terrorists, anti-government fighters, revolutionaries?). This can inevitably lead to bias as it is difficult not to apply a lens to something as contentious as conflict. Conflict resolution practitioners often do not document and share the choices that went into the collation of data, thereby perpetuating bias should this data be used in AI models.

Additionally, which data to collect and from where is a major hurdle. Take, for example, a hypothetical open source investigation of the offensive in northwest Syria that began May 2019 and is led by the Syrian Government. To collect violent incidences only from the Syrian government-owned Syria Arab News Agency means that most armed groups involved will be identified as "criminal gangs" or "terrorist" and aerial bombings will be drastically underreported. On the other hand, only using the Syrian Rebels Reddit thread will miss intra-opposition group fighting and atrocities that opposition groups may commit. Just as in for-profit market research, conflict analysis is much stronger when based on a variety of sources. Yet the answer to how can one amass enough conflict data from enough sources to decrease bias and include relevant detail is a difficult one for nonprofits to handle. Unlike for-profit data analytics teams, the conflict analysts crafting contextual briefings and stakeholder mapping for conflict resolution practitioners or humanitarians often do not have the manpower or expertise to manage multiple data flows on a large scale. Due to this difficulty, peacebuilders such as humanitarians and conflict resolution practitioners look to readily available and organized conflict datasets to address this issue for them. While convenient this introduces another question: what is the right data to inform the conflict analysis needed for the context an organization is working in? The localized nature of conflict data means that a methodology used to collate and analyze data in once context does not necessarily work in another. For example, think about the information that is needed to power the algorithms of self-driving cars. The traffic patterns and driver behaviors in San Francisco, California are quite different from those in Bogota, Colombia. This localized data makes it difficult to develop scalable AI solutions, a reality also seen in the conflict resolution world.

Since 2013 the Syria Conflict Mapping Project (SCMP) at the Carter Center has used publicly available, open source information to conduct detailed analysis on the Syrian conflict, in support of conflict resolution and humanitarian actors. This includes a database of 122,000 reported incidences of violence throughout Syria collected between 2013 and 2019 from YouTube, Twitter, Facebook, activist reporting websites, and local partner organizations. The Center was logging on average 400 events per week in 2015. Unable to maintain the cost of manually collecting and organizing conflict data for a high-volume area such as Syria, the Center began using ACLED's dataset in 2018 even though ACLED's data structure does not seamlessly mesh with its pre-existing conflict database. The Center consistently documents 13 different incident types of conflict-related events inside Syria: clashes, shelling, aerial bombardment, location capture, arrests/detention, suicide bomb, IED, landmine/UXO, sniper fire, assassination, protests, strategic developments, and violence against civilians. Conversely, ACLED organizes conflict event types into four broad categories with corresponding sub event types (Fig. 1).

This is a means to accommodate the range of conflicts ACLED collects data on. Additionally, ACLED does not document the multiple incident types that may be present in one violent incident report due to its hierarchy of incident types. Carter Center on the other hand often has listed two or three event types for a single violent incident report. The difference between these documentation methodologies means that analysts cannot compare Carter Center data and ACLED data all at once since conflict levels and incident type frequency will be skewed. Yet manual transformation of ACLED's Syria-related data, released on a weekly basis, takes on average 4 h per week due to the contextual nature of the data. An individual must be knowledgeable of the actors in the Syrian conflict, familiar with ACLED's collection methodology and resulting data structure, and well-versed in the Carter Center's conflict incident classification in order to understand what needs to be changed and how. As these parameters are replicated in other organizations across a variety of contexts, artificial intelligence, particularly supervised machine learning, has caught the attention

General	Event Type	Sub-Event Type
Violent events	Battles	Armed clash
		Government regains territory
		Non-state actor overtakes territory
	Explosions/Remote violence	Chemical weapon
		Air/drone strike
		Suicide bomb
		Shelling/artillery/missile attack
		Remote explosive/landmine/IED
		Grenade
	Violence against civilians	Sexual violence
		Attack
		Abduction/forced disappearance
Demonstrations	Protests	Peaceful protest
		Protest with intervention
		Excessive force against protesters
	Riots	Violent demonstration
		Mob violence
Non-violent actions	Strategic developments	Agreement
		Arrests
		Change to group/activity
		Disrupted weapons use
		Headquarters or base established
		Looting/property destruction
		Non-violent transfer of territory
		Other

Fig. 1 ACLED conflict event categories

of organizations working in the peace and security field. While natural language processing (NLP) is commonly used in marketing and advertising (such as crimson hexagon (Hitlinm P. 2015)), training NLP models to work with conflict data, especially information translated from one language to another, proves to be much more difficult.

In NLP, domain adaptation has traditionally been an important topic for syntactic parsing (McClosky et al. 2010) and named entity recognition (Chiticariu et al. 2010) among others. With the popularity of distributed representation, pre-trained word embedding models such as word2vec (Mikolov et al. 2013) and glove (Pennington et al. 2014) are also widely used for natural language tasks. For human beings, text comprehension is a basic task, performed daily. As early as in elementary school, we can read an article, and conclude about its key ideas and details. But for AI, full text comprehension is still an elusive goal. Added to this transliterated violent incident reporting and the inconsistent spelling and grammar that accompanies this, text comprehension is exceedingly difficult. Therefore, building machines that can perform text comprehension is of great interest. In this paper, we will focus on application of Deep Bidirectional Transformers for Language Understanding (BERT) (Devlin et al. 2018) to the problem of multi-label text classification.

Conflict resolution actors, conflict analysts, and the broader peace building field is unable to overcome the intensive time required to use publicly available conflict data in a responsible way. This often forces them to take publicly available conflict data "as is", rather than as a foundational dataset to be complemented by intentional data collection that forms the right dataset for a project. This lack of time, combined with a lack of data literacy, can lead to biased analysis and unwittingly incomplete datasets. By automating this event classification process, we can significantly reduce time spent on data preparation and provide a first step for conflict resolution practitioners to engage in intentional data preparation and collection. Additionally, conflict researchers would be able to spend more time understanding the trends and key insights needed to support their peace building and humanitarian efforts.

2.1 Data for This Work

The first version of the model is trained on Syria conflict data from ACLED between 2018 and 2019, totaling 7847 events. Since a single conflict event can contain multiple incident types, authors manually created a new row for each incident type while maintaining the unique ID of each conflict event (Figs. 2 and 3). This clearly identified the key words used to describe each incident type. This manual work resulted in 8942 conflict events detailing 11 different incident types, from which we used three (shelling, clashes, and strategic development) to train the NLP model.

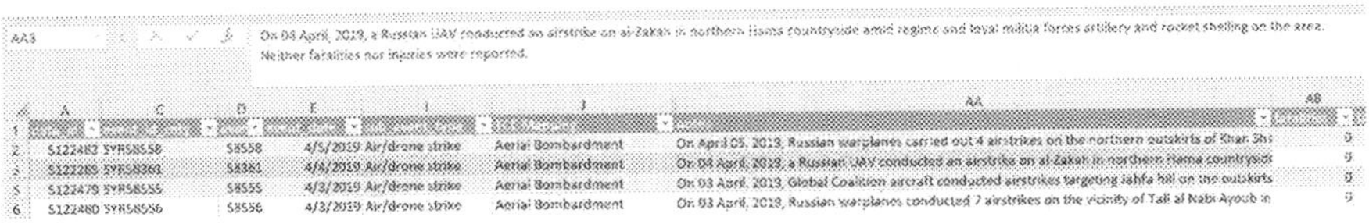

Fig. 2 Pre-data transformation

Fig. 3 Post data transformation

3 Method

Text Classification is a long-standing challenge in NLP, and the community has introduced several paradigms and datasets for the task over the past few years. These paradigms differ from each other in the type of text and labels, and the size of the training data, from a few hundreds to millions of examples. We are particularly interested in the context-aware text classification paradigm, where the label for each text snippet can be obtained by referring to its accompanying context (paragraph or a list of sentences). Research in the field of using pre-trained models have resulted in massive leap in state-of-the-art results for text classification. Some of the key milestones have been ELMo (Peters et al. 2018), ULMFiT (Howard and Ruder 2018) and OpenAI Transformer (Radford et al. 2018). All these approaches allow us to pre-train an unsupervised language model on large corpus of data such as all Wikipedia articles, and then fine-tune these pre-trained models on downstream tasks. However, the release of BERT (Devlin et al. 2018), a multilingual transformer-based model, has achieved state-of-the-art results, outperforming all the other models.

3.1 Why Use BERT?

Google Research recently open-sourced the TensorFlow implementation of BERT (Google 2019) and released six pre-trained models. BERT is a bidirectional model that is based on the transformer architecture and it replaces the sequential nature of Recurrent Neural Network (RNN) (Sherstinsky 2018) with a much faster attention-based approach (Vaswani et al. 2017). The BERT model is pre-trained on two unsupervised tasks, masked language modeling and next sentence prediction. This allows us to use a pre-trained BERT model and apply transfer learning and finetuning techniques for our problem.

3.2 Fine-tuning BERT for Multilabel Armed Conflict Event Classification

Modern machine learning models, especially deep neural networks, often significantly benefit from transfer learning. In computer vision, deep convolutional neural network (CNN) (Krizhevsky et al. 2012) trained on a large image classification dataset such as ImageNet (Deng et al. 2009) have proved to be useful for initializing models on other vision tasks (Yosinski et al. 2014). Researchers have shown the value of transfer learning using the trained neural network as the basis of a new purpose-specific model. In recent years, researchers have been showing that a similar technique can be useful in many natural language tasks. We use the smaller BERT

Base, uncased model as the base model for this paper. The BERT Base model has 12 attention layers and uses the word-piece-tokenizer (Wu et al. 2016), which converts all text to lowercase. We modify the BertForSequenceClassification class in BERT GitHub (Hugging-Face 2019) for multi-label classification. Figure 4 explains our multilabel classification pipeline. The training loop is identical to the one provided in run_classifier.py in Hugging-Face (2019). We train the model for 4 epochs with batch size of 16 and sequence length as 256. The learning rate is kept to 3e-5, as recommended for fine-tuning in the original BERT paper. We do not use the precision FP16 technique as binary-cross-entropy-with-logits loss function does not support FP16 processing.

4 Results

4.1 Prior Work

In conjunction with a team of students from Georgia Institute of Technology for a separate but overlapping project, authors tested the effectiveness of multiple, automated classification methods for transforming ACLED data to Carter Center conflict typology. Using data from the Carter Center's database, the ICT For Development Project team in Georgia Technology Institute (Michael 2019) vectorized data for each row in the "comments" column, containing a contextual description of the incident being documented. This helped to determine the word count vector and conduct further text processing, and label incident types with numerical codes per the Carter Center classification type. After separating 70% of the 8942 conflict events data into training data and the remaining 30% into test data, the team members experimented first with the Multinomial-Logit Model resulting in an evaluation accuracy of 88%. They then used a CNN model which produced an evaluation accuracy of 90%, but

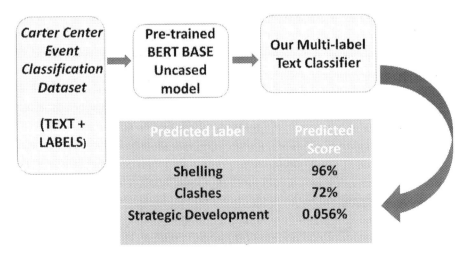

Fig. 4 BERT multi-label classification for carter center event classification

requiring long computing time to achieve the level of precision desired. To accomplish a single iteration of training, it took a CPU computer 1.5 h to complete. This combined with the need to train the model on multiple incident type categories made this method difficult for real-world application, particularly for nonprofits who do not have computers with expansive processing power. Lastly, the students tested the Multinomial Naïve Bayesian Model with an evaluation accuracy rate of 81%. While the Multinomial-Logit model was identified as the best option for text classification, the accuracy of the algorithm significantly decreased when applied to out-of-sample data, as ACLED data incident classification differs significantly from the Carter Center's incident classification.

4.2 Evaluation of Our Model

Out of the 8942 conflict events from 2018 to 2019, we used 80% for training and 20% for evaluating the model. The evaluation comprised of 1788 events from the dataset and had an accuracy of 96%. Figure 5a explains the ROC-AUC plot for our model, where class 0 is shelling events, class 1 is clashes events and class 2 is strategic development events. Figure 5b compares the evaluation accuracy of all prior work models versus our model .

To aid in the review of the output of our model, we created a data visualization using Power BI (Microsoft-PowerBI 2019) that facilitated the comparison of the predicted classifications versus the actual classifications of the evaluation set. This visualization simplified the data exploration and allowed authors to identify and examine misclassified points in an intuitive way. Figure 6 is a screen shot of the report with the legend of the map on the left displaying predicted classifications from our model and the legend of the map on the right displaying the actual classifications. The table in Fig. 6 shows the predicted classification label, predicted classification probability, and the text used for the prediction.

4.3 Out-of-Sample Evaluation of Our Model

The out-of-sample data consisted of 57,253 Syria conflict events from ACLED between 2017 and 2019, thereby including 31,393 conflict events from 2017

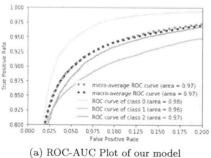
(a) ROC-AUC Plot of our model

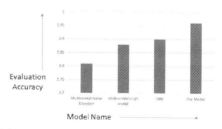
(b) Comparing evaluation accuracy of prior work models and our model

Fig. 5 Evaluation plots of our model

Armed Conflict Data in a Real-World Scenario...

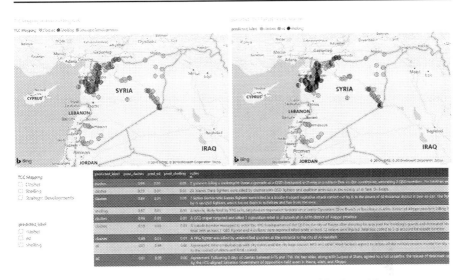

Fig. 6 Comparison of the predicted classifications versus the actual classifications of the test set

completely unseen by our model. Despite the variety of incident types in the test data set, our model had an accuracy rate of 90%. Experts manually reviewed the results of the out-of-sample data, dividing our results into four thresholds:

- incidences given a probability higher than 85% of being the incident type identified by ACLED
- incidences given probabilities between 75 and 85%
- incidences less than 75%
- incidences given a probability higher than 85% for an incident type not identified by ACLED.

These thresholds were used to group results by incident type (as shown in Fig. 7) for a human analyst to review. Figure 7a,b,c shows the breakdown of our model's classification of out-of-sample 57,000 conflict events based on the three incident types it was trained on: shelling, clashes, and strategic developments. For example, in Fig. 7a, the largest grouping of results for the incident types shelling was those identified as shelling by ACLED and given an 85% probability by our model as being shelling. Figure 7d,e,f shows the breakdown of our model's classification on 2017 conflict events only, based on the three incident types it was trained on: shelling, clashes, and strategic developments. For example, in Fig. 7d, the largest grouping of results for the incident types shelling was those identified as shelling by ACLED and given an 85% probability by our model as being shelling.

5 Impact

Results for an expected outcome (such as BERT giving a 90% probability of being "shelling" to violent events identified as shelling by ACLED) were reviewed for 1000

A. Trivedi et al.

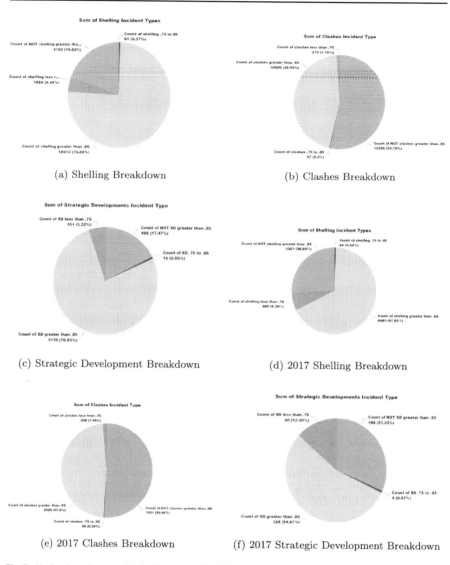

Fig. 7 Evaluation of our model: incident types breakdown

samples. This was a simple confirmation that the model was agreeing with the classification of an event given by ACLED or Carter Center staff. Abnormal results on the other hand were reviewed more thoroughly by those familiar with data. Abnormal results were when BERT disagreed with the conflict event classification provided by ACLED analysts. Overall, our model identified conflict incidences that should have more than one incident type. For example, our model gave 270 conflict events identified by ACLED as clashes a probability of 75% or less of being clashes. Rather than this being an inaccuracy, our model accurately identified that 105 of these events were also shelling. A consistent trend in conflict events in Syria are that clashes and shelling often accompany each other, a trend that Carter Center had started manually documenting by inputting multiple incident types into one conflict event. Conflict activity composed of other incident types that was not trained in the model, such as air/drone attack, were often classified as shelling or clashes. For example, of the 4782 incidents given an 85% probability or higher by our model as being shelling, despite not identified as shelling by ACLED, 4388 of these were air/drone attacks according to ACLED's typology. In searching through these, the authors found that 1374 of incidents contain the word "shell" pointing to the likelihood that many of the conflict incidents are multi-incident types. This aligns with the trends of the conflict as air/drone attacks are of- ten accompanied by on the ground shelling as well as aerial shelling. Often language used to describe an air/drone attack includes words such as "targeted" and "artillery", which is like descriptions of conflict activity involving shelling. Our model has successfully been able to identify the above trends from the context hidden in text data. Thus, we can conclude that use of this model would be able to save Carter Center many hours of manual data preprocessing task. Sample code and data for this work is provided in footnote below[1]

Open source conflict reporting is often not structured in a way to facilitate automation, making visualization and analysis of conflict data a time intensive process. While ACLED is among the leaders of publicly available, structured conflict data, the contextual nature of this type of information means there is no one size that fits all. Using automation to speed up the manual transformation of conflict data gives the nonprofit practitioners more time to conduct the analysis essential to their work and access an array of conflict datasets, which can lower reporting bias through a diversification of data sources. Automation gives them more time to engage in intentional data collection, which builds a more robust conflict dataset. Lastly, and more broadly, our model contributes to the gradual trend of integrating technology and the peace building and conflict resolution sector as practitioners recognize the potential impact of the digital age on their work.

6 Future Work

Human supervision is an integral part of our model due to the nature of transliterated conflict event reporting. Focusing on this model, the authors review the challenges of using conflict data and the opportunity for further training of the model. Our model clearly indicates that we can identify the context of a conflict event and can thus identify conflict events that should have multiple incident types. This opens options to expand the model's incident category to most the Carter Center's incident types. This will allow our model to accurately classify more incident types according to the Carter Center's typology and provide higher probabilities for multiple incident types with minimal human supervision.

In practice, this means that Carter Center staff can rely on this algorithm to spend a few minutes a week reclassifying the incident types in ACLED's data so they can

---

[1] https://tinyurl.com/y5cs65dx

see the trends in the conflict that are overlooked by ACLED's incident type hierarchy approach. Staff can see that, for example, an incident occurring in a particular place and time includes the detonation of two IEDs, a suicide bomb, and shelling, providing a detailed documentation of the type of violence carried out in a single event. ACLED's incident type hierarchy would only log one of those events in its database, thereby overlooking low-level events that can hint at a deteriorating security environment that can affect the work of conflict resolution practitioners and humanitarians. It also significantly misrepresents nature of the conflict and its historical representation through documentation. The Carter Center's Syria team is training an expanded version of model 1 that will be tested in the team's database environment and integrated in to their data workflow. Team members look forward to the ability to produce impactful analysis for their work without having to spend hours each week piecing apart the data. This current time commitment restricts the type of analysis they can provide to humanitarians and their conflict resolution colleagues. Authors intend to share knowledge from this work with other practitioners who need more accurate conflict data but struggle with the time demand, thereby contributing to the integration of technology in the peace building sector.

References

ACLED (2019). https://www.acleddata.com/data/.
Chiticariu, L., Krishnamurthy, R., Li, Y., Reiss, F., Vaithyanathan, S. (2010). Domain adaptation of rule-based annotators for named-entity recognition tasks. In *Proceedings of the 2010 Conference on Empirical Methods in Natural Language Processing, EMNLP '10, Association for Computational Linguistics, Stroudsburg, PA, USA* (pp. 1002–1012). http://dl.acm.org/citation.cfm?id=1870658.1870756.
Deng, J., Dong, W., Socher, R., Li, L.J., Li, K., Fei-Fei, L. (2009). Imagenet: a large-scale hierarchical image database. In *CVPR09*.
Devlin, J., Chang, M.W., Lee, K., Toutanova, K. (2018). BERT: pre-training of deep bidirectional transformers for language understanding. arXiv:1810.04805.
Dupuy, K., & Rustad, S. (2018). Trends in armed conflict.
Google (2019). Bert https://github.com/google-research/bert.
Hitlinm P. (2015). Methodology: how crimson hexagon works.
Howard, J., & Ruder, S. (2018). Universal language model fine-tuning for text classification. arXiv:1801.06146.
Hugging-Face (2019). Bert pytorch https://github.com/huggingface/pytorch-transformers.
Krizhevsky, A., Sutskever, I., Hinton, G.E. (2012). Imagenet classification with deep convolutional neural networks. In Pereira, F., Burges, C.J.C., Bottou, L., Weinberger, K.Q. (Eds.) *Advances in Neural Information Processing Systems 25. Curran Associates, Inc.* (pp. 1097–1105). http://papers.nips.cc/paper/4824-imagenet-classification-with-deep-convolutional-neural-networks.pdf.
McClosky, D., Charniak, E., Johnson, M. (2010). Automatic domain adaptation for parsing. In *Human Language Technologies: The 2010 Annual Conference of the North American Chapter of the Association for Computational Linguistics, Association for Computational Linguistics, Los Angeles, California* (pp. 28–36). https://www.aclweb.org/anthology/N10-1004.
Michael (2019). ICT for development project, Georgia Technology Intitute. https://mikeb.inta.gatech.edu/research (Best).
Microsoft-PowerBI (2019). Power BI. https://powerbi.microsoft.com/en-us/.
Mikolov, T., Chen, K., Corrado, G., Dean, J. (2013). Efficient estimation of word representations in vector space. arXiv:1301.3781.
Pennington, J., Socher, R., Manning, C.D. (2014). Glove: global vectors for word representation. In *Proceedings of the 2014 Conference on Empirical Methods in Natural Language Processing (EMNLP)* (pp. 1532–1543).

Peters, M.E., Neumann, M., Iyyer, M., Gardner, M., Clark, C., Lee, K., Zettlemoyer, L. (2018). Deep contextualized word representations. arXiv:1802.05365.

Radford, A., Narasimhan, K., Salimans, T., Sutskever, I. (2018). Improving language understanding by generative pre-training. Forthcoming.

Raleigh, C., Linke, A., Hegre, H., Karlsen, J. (2010). Introducing acled: an armed conflict location and event dataset: Special data feature. *Journal of Peace Research, 47*, 651–660. https://doi.org/10.1177/0022343310378914.

Sherstinsky, A. (2018). Fundamentals of Recurrent Neural Network (RNN) and Long Short-Term Memory (LSTM) network. arXiv:1808.03314.

Tufekci, Z., & Wilson, C. (2012). Social media and the decision to participate in political protest: Observations from Tahrir Square.

UN-Peacemaker (2019). Mediation support digital toolkit. https://peacemaker.un.org/digitaltoolkit.

Vaswani, A., Shazeer, N., Parmar, N., Uszkoreit, J., Jones, L., Gomez, A.N., Kaiser, L., Polosukhin, I. (2017). Attention is all you need. In *Proceedings of the 31st Conference on Neural Information Processing Systems.*

Wu, Y., Schuster, M., Chen, Z., Le, Q.V., Norouzi, M., Macherey, W., Krikun, M., Cao, Y., Gao, Q., Macherey, K., Klingner, J., Shah, A., Johnson, M., Liu, X., Kaiser, Ł., Gouws, S., Kato, Y., Kudo, T., Kazawa, H., Stevens, K., Kurian, G., Patil, N., Wang, W., Young, C., Smith, J., Riesa, J., Rudnick, A., Vinyals, O., Corrado, G., Hughes, M., Dean, J. (2016). Google's Neural Machine Translation System: Bridging the Gap between Human and Machine Translation. arXiv:1609.08144.

Yosinski, J., Clune, J., Bengio, Y., Lipson, H. (2014). How transferable are features in deep neural networks? In *Proceedings of the 28th Conference on Neural Information Processing Systems.*

Publisher's Note Springer Nature remains neutral with regard to jurisdictional claims in published maps and institutional affiliations.

Affiliations

Anusua Trivedi[1] ⓘ **· Kate Keator[2] · Michael Scholtens[2] · Brandon Haigood[2] · Rahul Dodhia[1] · Juan Lavista Ferres[1] · Ria Sankar[1] · Avirishu Verma[1]**

Kate Keator
kate.keator@cartercenter.org

Michael Scholtens
Michael.Scholtens@cartercenter.org

Brandon Haigood
brandon.haigood@cartercenter.org

Rahul Dodhia
radodhia@microsoft.com

Juan Lavista Ferres
jlavista@microsoft.com

Ria Sankar
rias@microsoft.com

Avirishu Verma
Avirishu.Verma@microsoft.com

[1]   Microsoft, 1 Microsoft Way, Redmond, WA, 98052, USA

[2]   The Carter Center, 453 Freedom Parkway, Atlanta, GA, 30307, USA